The LITA Leadership Guide

LIBRARY INFORMATION TECHNOLOGY ASSOCIATION (LITA) GUIDES

Marta Mestrovic Deyrup, Ph.D.
Acquisitions Editor, Library Information and Technology Association,
a division of the American Library Association

The Library Information Technology Association (LITA) Guides provide information and guidance on topics related to cutting-edge technology for library and IT specialists.

Written by top professionals in the field of technology, the guides are sought after by librarians wishing to learn a new skill or to become current in today's best practices.

Each book in the series has been overseen editorially since conception by LITA and reviewed by LITA members with special expertise in the specialty area of the book.

Established in 1966, the Library and Information Technology Association (LITA) is the division of the American Library Association (ALA) that provides its members and the library and information science community as a whole with a forum for discussion, an environment for learning, and a program for actions on the design, development, and implementation of automated and technological systems in the library and information science field.

Approximately 25 LITA Guides were published by Neal-Schuman and ALA between 2007 and 2015. Rowman & Littlefield took over publication of the series beginning in late 2015. Books in the series published by Rowman & Littlefield are:

Digitizing Flat Media: Principles and Practices
The Librarian's Introduction to Programming Languages
Library Service Design: A LITA Guide to Holistic Assessment, Insight, and Improvement
Data Visualization: A Guide to Visual Storytelling for Librarians
Mobile Technologies in Libraries: A LITA Guide
Innovative LibGuides Applications
Integrating LibGuides into Websites
Protecting Patron Privacy: A LITA Guide
The LITA Leadership Guide: The Librarian as Entrepreneur, Leader, and Technologist

The LITA Leadership Guide

The Librarian as Entrepreneur, Leader, and Technologist

Edited by
Carl Antonucci
Sharon Clapp

Foreword by Maureen Sullivan

ROWMAN & LITTLEFIELD
Lanham • Boulder • New York • London

Published by Rowman & Littlefield
A wholly owned subsidiary of The Rowman & Littlefield Publishing Group, Inc.
4501 Forbes Boulevard, Suite 200, Lanham, Maryland 20706
www.rowman.com

Unit A, Whitacre Mews, 26-34 Stannary Street, London SE11 4AB

British Library Cataloguing in Publication Information Available

Library of Congress Cataloging-in-Publication Data Available

ISBN 9781442279018 (hardback : alk. paper) | ISBN 9781442279025 (pbk. : alk. paper) | ISBN 9781442279032 (electronic)

♾ ™ The paper used in this publication meets the minimum requirements of American National Standard for Information Sciences Permanence of Paper for Printed Library Materials, ANSI/NISO Z39.48-1992.

Printed in the United States of America

For my wife, Luisa, and my children, Natalie, Antonio, and David.
—Carl Antonucci

With gratitude to my dear husband, Chris Michaud, who has been my strength in all of our years together.
—Sharon Clapp

Contents

Foreword

Maureen Sullivan

Librarians have long recognized the need to pursue innovation to ensure that the programs and services offered to students, faculty, and scholars meet their ever-changing needs and expectations. The evolving digital world brings new challenges and calls for every librarian to develop as a leader, entrepreneur, and technologist. The confluence of these three areas of practice demands a renewed commitment to professional development and a disciplined approach to learning a set of new competencies. The professional practice of librarians is becoming more complex. It brings challenges and also opportunities. To embrace and carry out the three roles of entrepreneur, leader, and technologist requires a clear and deep understanding of the knowledge, skills, and abilities that are essential to effective practice. The future of academic and research libraries and that of our profession depends upon this commitment.

The librarian as entrepreneur is a role rich with opportunities to make a difference in higher education and to make a significant contribution to student learning, faculty teaching, research, and scholarship. The entrepreneur recognizes that creativity is a capacity in all of us and takes steps to nurture this in self and others. This leads to innovation in practice when collaboration and experimentation become a way of life in professional practice. The librarian as entrepreneur embraces opportunities to rethink current practice, to create new programs and services, to rethink and redesign.

The librarian as leader is an essential role, both inside the library organization and in the larger external environment. Every librarian needs to be a leader whether by the formal requirements of her or his position in the library or through more informal situations where leadership is undertaken because opportunities present themselves. Both formal and informal leaders must have the capacity to engage, inspire, and motivate those with whom they work. They need to have strong interpersonal skills, especially the ability to communicate and manage relationships with a variety of diverse individuals. Leaders need to have emotional intelligence; be willing to take risks and pursue new initiatives and areas of work; deal with different constituencies and manage their different expectations; articulate a compelling vision while engaging others to work together to create a shared vision; and foster a work environment in which diversity, inclusion, collaboration, future-focus, and high performance define the organizational culture.

The librarian as technologist role is one that challenges some, especially those who are beyond midcareer. This role is as important and critical to successful organizational performance as the other two. The time has come for every librarian to have a general knowledge of the key technology systems and applications in libraries and to possess the core skills of the technologist. As we move further and deeper into the digital world every competent professional must be committed to keeping up with the key trends and developments in this area. This may be a challenging area for individual professional development, but it also is an area that is essential for personal mastery in our field.

The successful integration of these three roles throughout the field will enable the collaboration and commitment necessary to rethink and redesign our work, our organizational structures, facility and space design, service models, and what it will mean to be a librarian in the academy of the future. The contributions of librarians to higher education often go unnoticed and underappreciated. It is time to step forward and embrace the roles of entrepreneur, leader, and technologist and to do so in collaboration with colleagues in our libraries and across the field.

Read these chapters to learn from the experience of the authors and to consider where there might be applications for you in your own practice. Also look for ideas about initiatives to pursue in your library. Use this to identify steps and strategies to strengthen your role as a librarian who successfully integrates the three functions of entrepreneur, leader, and technologist. Work with colleagues to ensure that our academic and research libraries continue to support student learning, faculty teaching, research, and scholarship as the world around us evolves and brings new challenges and opportunities.

Preface

Operating in a time of disruptive change and innovation, libraries require skilled, agile, technology-driven leadership in order to survive and thrive. This book brings together three important professional development topics—leadership, entrepreneurship, and technology—in one volume, uniting theory, practice, and case studies from experienced colleagues in the field. The American Library Association has started a new initiative called Libraries Transform. One of the main ideas of this initiative is to show that the twenty-first-century library is less about the physical resources that they have always provided for people and more about the value of librarians and how they engage with the people in the communities where they work.

Librarians today provide added value to the patrons they serve by the five key areas (education, employment, entrepreneurship, empowerment, and engagement) of the Libraries Transform initiative. In order to ensure that libraries satisfy the twenty-first-century learning and research needs of its community of learners, librarians are involved in innovative programs and initiatives that would have never taken place in the traditional libraries of the past. The editors of this guide work in an academic library that is undergoing a vast transformation and have witnessed firsthand how librarians as leaders, entrepreneurs, and technologists have successfully worked with the members of our university community by facilitating knowledge creation and inspiring lifelong learning. This guide will enhance the traditional library leadership literature by highlighting how skills in leadership, entrepreneurship, and technology are necessary platform skills for librarians working at all levels during these disruptive times. It will also show how experienced colleagues have successfully created positive changes for themselves, their patrons, and their libraries as leaders, entrepreneurs, and technologists in the changing libraries of the twenty-first century.

Introduction

This book demonstrates some of the many ways that librarians are rising to the challenge of their times and building new ways forward through their leadership capacity, entrepreneurial approaches, and technological acumen.

Part 1 of this book brings together three different views of the "librarian as leader." Bradford Eden starts us off with his chapter on lessons learned in leadership over the course of his career as a library director. He discusses the particular and personal challenges of managing staff, as well as many other topics important to leaders at all levels, such as risk taking, visioning, marketing and outreach, assessment, and mentoring.

In chapter 2, Georgia Institute of Technology librarians Emy Nelson Decker, Marlee Givens, and Bruce Henson demonstrate the leadership required to implement a new service model in their discussion of the library's "roving reference" pilot project. Finally, Hong Ma, of the Loyola University Chicago Libraries, shows how the role of systems librarian has evolved into a key leadership position as "an architect of technology infrastructure" in chapter 3.

Mary Scanlon and Michael Crumpton open our section on the "librarian as entrepreneur" by discussing the ways that librarianship has long supported entrepreneurs in our society and how librarians themselves are now taking to heart many of the ideas that characterize the entrepreneurial endeavor, such as encouraging experimentation and building community. They discuss the Conference for Entrepreneurial Librarians that their home institutions created several years ago in North Carolina and the work that has resulted from this focus on entrepreneurship in libraries.

In chapter 5, Rebecca Bichel and C. Heather Scalf discuss how the University of Texas at Arlington (UTA) Libraries took the notion of "disruptive change" to the heart of the organization where it has led to innovation in the provision of library services and changes in organizational structure to support that innovation.

Finally, in chapter 6 the University of Connecticut's Michael Rodriguez brings us a fascinating look at how workspace can encourage the innovation in any organization and how this may apply to libraries.

Junior Tidal's discussion of "the promise and perils of open source" technology for libraries opens the final part of the book, which is devoted to the "librarian as technologist." Tidal provides an extensive scan of the open source software ecosystem that has developed to support many library functions while pointing out the challenges of deploying nonproprietary software.

Caitlin Bagley, from Gonzaga University, discusses the adoption and abandonment of technology, illustrating these possibilities with a comparative discussion of two specific tools that were used with varying degrees of success by the reference and instructional librarians at her institution.

Harish Maringanti concludes this book with his proposal of a model to align academic libraries' strategies with their technological and organizational structures. He brings a perspective strongly grounded in the worlds of IT and business to bear on his experience in libraries and how this way of thinking could increase the library's effectiveness as an organization.

This book serves as an example of how members of a field with a diversity of perspectives and experiences can share and learn from one another. This sharing is crucial for our success, particularly in these times of extraordinary change and the pressures that result from this change. The contributing authors have been generous with their time, their words, and their openness, by sharing their projects, their aspirations, and yes, even the "failures" that have led them to the pivots of taking on new tactics, while abandoning old ones. We are grateful to them because we know that we are more powerful when we build upon the work and knowledge of our colleagues.

We are proud to offer this compilation into the body of literature on librarianship. Today, the librarian takes on many roles, serving as leader, entrepreneur, and technologist in the course of moving our libraries and our field forward to meet the changing needs of today's society.

Part I

Leadership

Chapter One

What It Means to Be a Leader in Academic Libraries in the Twenty-First Century

Bradford Lee Eden

When you succeed, I succeed.—Ken Bierman

Early in my academic library career, I was fortunate enough to have a tried and proven library leader as my supervisor. Ken Bierman was at the end of a long and satisfying career when he became director of knowledge management at the UNLV Libraries in 1999. I started as head of cataloging a month after Ken, and was placed into a very challenging job with a number of difficult situations that needed to be resolved in a short time span: moving into a new $58 million library, a large backlog of current print serial titles in cataloging for which there was no room in the new library, and being a tenure-track department head supervising three tenured librarians. Not the most ideal of situations for a new librarian. Ken immediately took me under his wing, indicating that the changes that needed to be made would be a team effort, as his tenured status ensured that decisions coming from him would not affect my tenure-track status in any way, since I was just implementing his directions. Under Ken's guidance, I was able to accomplish the impossible, get the serials backlog in control, and obtain tenure. Ken used the quote above numerous times during his time at UNLV, taking not only myself but his other direct reports under his mentorship, from which we all benefited and now prosper in numerous ways. I still use many of Ken's techniques and attitudes, both as a leader and as a mentor: his "management by food" philosophy, his openness and ability to hear all sides of an important decision, and especially his support for professional development and training for both librarians and library staff in new skill sets and job duties.

The quote at the beginning is simple yet powerful, and it has provided the basis for my own management and leadership style. Library managers and leaders have a duty and obligation to assist those whom they lead and manage to be successful, whether that involves emotional support, mission and vision support, and especially professional development support. In a time when academic libraries must be flexible, innovative, mobile, nimble, and collaborative in everything that they do, it is imperative that librarians and library staff be provided the emotional and financial support to learn and grow in the new job duties and responsibilities that we are asking them to take on and direct. These jobs are very different than the ones they currently occupy and for which many of them began their careers, and part of a library leader's challenge is assisting in the process of asking, directing, and then providing the needed training and support for our librarians and staff to adapt and move into these new services and jobs. As Ken's quote so aptly states, when one's librarians and library staff are provided with the necessary support and training to do the jobs that we ask them to do, not only do they succeed, but we succeed as their supervisors, and this is what academic faculty and university administration see in a library that is functioning properly and working collaboratively within their organizational structure. Successful librarians and library staff, working to provide the needed services within the organization, reflect their success back to the library leader at the helm. Since Ken's retirement in 2006, I have been able to use his mentorship and leadership ideas in numerous other situations and job opportunities, and this simple quote has never let me down.

The purpose of this chapter is to summarize some of the lessons learned in my twenty-plus years as a library administrator. I don't claim to know it all, nor have I always been successful in the projects or with the people that I have encountered during that time period (I am sure that I am not alone in this), but I feel that I can contribute my knowledge and experience with others who are on the same path and looking for mentorship and guidance. As such, here are my thoughts regarding library leadership.

PLENTY OF LITERATURE TO HELP YOU

There are many books on library management and leadership available, many of them recent additions to the literature. I have published in this area (*Leadership in Academic Libraries Today*, edited with Jody Condit Fagan [2014], and the Creating the 21st-Century Academic Library series [2015–2016]), but I have to say that the most influential book that I have found is Susan Curzon's *What Every Library Director Should Know* (2014). Susan's book comes from her years of experience as dean of libraries at California State University, Northridge, and is written in a style that is blunt, informative, and commonsense. Her down-to-earth advice is primarily focused on her own experiences at the leadership position itself, rather than on theories, training tips, and workbook exercises. Here are some of her main points, which are so important to remember when you are a library dean or university librarian:

- Politics is everything
- Customer number one—your boss
- Knowing your faculty senate
- Engaging all staff, and knowing the players (she discusses many of these roles)
- How to work in a unionized environment
- Dealing with the borders of the realm (friends groups, community groups, student associations, etc.)
- How to deal with a death in the library
- Attempting change management
- Various transitions in your life (being fired, retiring, resigning, promotion, etc.)

Of course there are many good books out there, but I have found Susan's book the best one for my career (see references for other good resources).

COMMUNICATION

Probably the biggest challenge for any leader is communication; you have to do it all the time, and you can't do it enough. I have tried to set up all-staff meetings at least twice a year, in order to let everyone know what is happening politically within the university, especially related to compensation and student enrollment. I always use the analogy that location, location, location is the mantra in real estate, and I think that the mantra for any manager or leader has to be communication, communication, communication. I think that the worst thing that can happen to anyone in the workplace is being left out of the loop: hearing important news about library job changes, life situations, and especially changes and new directions within the library through the grapevine is what isolates and demeans library workers the most. It is key that a library leader constantly communicate, gather, and share information as much as possible, and involve librarians and library staff in making the key decisions and strategic plan of the library. And setting the tone is key: the library isn't mine, the library isn't yours or ours, the library belongs to the people to whom we offer our services and resources. In that sense, we are the facilitators and enablers of where our patrons and our administration want to go and where they want to be. Communication needs to be lateral and vertical, from the president or chancellor to dining services, from the students to the academic faculty. Everyone needs to be part of the process in determining the directions and services that the library offers, both short term and long term. Which takes us to the next section.

MANAGED RISK TAKING

Librarians work in a profession that holds on to legacy practices and work-flows, and has challenges with trying new services and technologies and taking risks. One way that I have found to alleviate this mind-set is to implement a culture of exploration and managed risk taking; that is, everything should be a pilot project. For instance, in my current position, I purchased an older version of a 3D Visbox from the College of Engineering, in order to explore gaming and digital humanities outreach to faculty and students. As much as possible, have the organization try new technologies and services, and lead by supporting this culture of innovation through initial funding and professional development. If something works, fantastic—pour more funding and professional development into it. If it doesn't work, then get out of it as quickly as possible and move on to another new experiment or service. In this way, everyone understands that it is about trying new things and seeing whether it makes a difference. In the end, people are rewarded for brain-storming and investing time in innovation, and if things don't work out, there isn't a fear of retaliation or failure because the organization moves on to more exploration and innovation.

VISIONING/STRATEGIC PLANNING

This really is the lead role of a library dean/director, and one that requires balance and finesse. The vision for the organization needs to come from the top, but the implementation of objectives, goals, and action items comes from the people themselves. And when doing strategic planning, it is not about what or where the library organization wants to go or be. In the back of my mind and when doing strategic planning, I always remind everyone: this is the library of this institution and its constituencies (students, faculty, staff, and administration). We need to constantly be attuned to the needs and directions of our patrons, and both anticipate and influence the strategic plans of the institution and align ourselves with those plans first and foremost. After all, that is where the money comes from. One very direct and informal approach to obtain student opinions is by setting up whiteboards around the library, especially near entrances, and placing a specific question on it and seeing how the students respond. For the students, who are posting constantly on various social media websites, this approach is successful because it is both quick and anonymous.

Strategic planning can no longer be something that we do once every two to five years, and then put the plan on the shelf and move forward. But it also cannot be something that drains an organization of its time, motivation, and overall mood; we are all doing more with less, and have jobs that need to get done. For this approach to be successful, it needs to be a key job duty of the dean/university librarian. Understanding where we are, where we need to be, and how to get there, however, needs to be constantly discussed, negotiated, planned, and worked toward. This is why I have learned that strategic planning needs to be: (1) iterative (done yearly), (2) unobtrusive (does not take away unnecessarily from people's time and work), (3) inclusive (involves everyone in the organization who wishes to participate), (4) transparent (everyone can see all steps of the process), and (5) in alignment with the institution's strategic plan (for obvious reasons). Once this pattern of iterative strategic planning is established, the organizational culture becomes adapted to a constant discussion around objectives and action items that are short term and measurable, with negotiated lines of responsibility within the organization. It also allows the organization to try new services and ideas without long-term consequences if objectives are not met. I have also found that sharing information on the status of objectives and action items halfway through a fiscal year reminds everyone that strategic planning is not an exercise in futility but an actual process that is being monitored and implemented on a regular basis. Obviously it helps if the institution itself has an iterative strategic planning process in place as well, but if it doesn't, this is a way that the library can model strategic planning that is active, manageable, and workable for the rest of the campus (Eden, forthcoming).

MANAGEMENT BY FOOD

This particular management technique I picked up from my mentor Ken Bierman, and I have used it in every administrative position that I have been in. Basically, it goes like this: for my direct reports, we have a monthly meeting to connect and share information and discuss larger organizational issues. This meeting is a lunch meeting, off campus, that I pay for. In this way, those who report directly to me get a free lunch, get away from the work environment to a stress-free location, and get time with their peers and colleagues. I get a chance to work with my direct reports in a stress-free and easy atmosphere, can share and discuss important information without being in a sterile office, and get a break on my taxes. Thus far, I have found that this technique works well all around, and my direct reports really appreciate the fact that their boss takes them out to lunch.

Within the larger library organization, I have also instituted informal gatherings such as potluck lunches that are held throughout the year for everyone, as well as formal events such as end-of-the-semester lunch functions that are catered as well as an annual picnic for librarians and library staff. Many library deans/directors do this, but many do not understand how important this is to the overall morale and mood of the library organization, and how essential these functions can be as stress reducers as well as times for those on the front and back lines to interact with their dean/director. Sometimes it is the smallest of investments in time and money that produce the largest overall results (this is apparent in many other instances as well).

ORGANIZATIONAL CULTURE AND HUMAN RESOURCES

One of the many dynamics in library organizations is the mix of statuses and representations of library employees, which can have a tremendous effect on the openness and rate of change that can occur regarding the development of new services and job duties/responsibilities. These dynamics include whether the librarians are considered academic faculty (tenure-track/tenured), have a parallel ladder similar to academic faculty (mirrors tenure-track/tenured but not exactly the same), or are considered staff. Unionized environments also have a definite influence on how a library dean/director can implement change in the library, and this also depends on who is unionized (library staff, librarians, and/or both). I have worked in a number of environments, from no union representation to four unions in the library, from librarians as tenured faculty to librarians without tenure. It is definitely a challenging balancing act to say the least, and while change can be implemented in any environment, a library dean/director needs to understand and work within the organizational culture first and foremost before any kind of change management strategy moves forward. This is where some of the other topics, such as iterative strategic planning and managed risk taking, can provide the balance needed to help the library organization plan and manage the change needed to stay viable and innovative within the larger institutional organization.

BE SUCCESSFUL WITH WHAT YOU HAVE/DON'T COMPLAIN ABOUT WHAT YOU DON'T HAVE

This was an interesting lesson that I learned early in my career. I had just been hired as a second-in-command at a very large academic library, and my immediate boss was leaving to take another position. It became apparent that there was a strong tension between the university librarian and the chancellor regarding the library budget and lack of inflationary and other increases for a number of years, and that the university librarian was strongly critical of this situation to the chancellor and to other high-level administrators and academic faculty. As a result, it was fairly well known that the chancellor had come to ignore and isolate the university librarian privately while supporting the library publicly.

This lesson learned, along with Susan Curzon's admonition that a library dean/director should focus on being successful with the funds and resources that one has, rather than focusing on what one doesn't have, has helped to guide me both as a library leader as well as assisting others within the library organization regarding the political and economic ramifications of how one responds (both privately and publicly) to the resources and monies granted by the larger institution to the library. Every dean wishes that they had more, as does every provost, as does every president/chancellor; the reality is that there are limited funds that need to be distributed throughout the institution, and complaining about what you haven't received doesn't really address the question that a provost/president wants answered: What are you doing with what you have, and are you being successful with that? What speaks louder than any words is whether you are running your organization effectively, and implementing new services and innovations that matter to the faculty and students, and that they are your ambassadors to higher administration regarding your success in those endeavors. When higher administration sees (and hears from faculty and students) that the library is doing a fantastic job, and is offering this service or that focus that really matters to them, then they become your advocates for more resources and funds; in the end, it goes back to the iterative strategic planning, the managed risk taking, and constantly having your fingers on the pulse of those who are important to higher administration (namely, faculty and students). When the library dean/director complains about not having enough resources, it is just another dean in a long line complaining to the provost; but when faculty and students tell the provost and the president about how the library has helped them be successful in their classrooms and with their studies, then the library doesn't have to do anything: the resources and funds will follow. Success breeds more success, and goes back to the opening quote (paraphrased): when the library succeeds, then the provost/president succeeds. It is a cycle that every person in academic administration wants to be in, and is much more comfortable (and less stressful) to work in than constantly complaining.

MARKETING/OUTREACH

The idea of both the library (whether public or academic) and higher education as a "public good" went away after the 2008 economic recession. It is quite apparent that thinking that people understand the importance of libraries, or know that the library is more than just a warehouse of books, is wishful thinking. Just like the adage "You have to market yourself," today's library needs to carefully and thoughtfully strategize and prioritize the way that it markets and presents itself to its constituents. No one is going to do it for us (unless we ask them to, or our services reflect the success of our faculty and students; see above); therefore, strategic planning surrounding marketing and outreach is crucial for academic library leaders. While most cannot afford to hire a marketing firm or even a marketing person, you can put together a marketing/outreach committee led by someone in administration or by a key librarian with a background or interest in communication and outreach. As the library experiments and innovates with new services and technologies, it is essential that they are marketed and featured in prominent print and online publications. In addition, having a strong social media presence that is constantly monitored and juxtaposed to highlight new digitized collections, services of interest to faculty and students, and timely news and offerings related to critical dates on the calendar (finals week, spring break, beginning of a semester, etc.) is very important. In short, this needs to be a priority for a library dean/director; otherwise, everything that you do that is positive and important will never be known or acknowledged.

"IT'S ALL ABOUT DATA"/ASSESSMENT

The pressure to verify and authenticate broad-based and specific statements on the performance of, opinion of, effect of, and evidence of the library's influence on the institution's concern regarding the recruitment and retention of students has become a high priority for any library dean/director. While libraries have always been good at collecting data, they haven't been very good at presenting or summarizing or even linking library data points to the institution's priorities or objectives. Make no mistake: the institution's highest priority in the current climate is (1) the recruitment of students and (2) the retention of same students. It costs a lot of money to recruit students; the investment to retain students doesn't come close to the costs of recruiting them, which is why retention efforts are so crucial. So for the library to actively and openly illustrate how it recruits and retains students through its data and assessment of its activities, services, and surveys is key to its survival and growth. In my current situation, I initiated a task force on assessment first, which then gained some in-house experience with LibQUAL and other initiatives, so that a formal library committee was able to be standardized. Again, iterative strategic planning with actionable and measurable goals is the best way to show the importance of this work within the library organization, and it is imperative for the library dean/director to showcase this data and assessment whenever possible to higher administration, faculty, and students.

MENTORING/PROFESSIONAL SUPPORT

Internal to the library, a key role that the library dean/director needs to take the lead on is the mentoring of librarians and library staff, and providing the funds necessary for professional development. Paying for leadership opportunities, whether through webinars or attendance at specific leadership institutes, is a small price to pay for helping people to grow, learn, and reach their full potential in the organization and in future jobs that they will aspire to. Maintaining a culture of encouragement, support (both emotional and financial), and especially interest in the well-being and skill sets of all of your employees will provide the basis for assisting them to innovate and envision themselves and their work into the future. We can't ask librarians and library staff to do new jobs or acquire skill sets without providing them with the financial and training support necessary for them to be successful; to do otherwise defies common sense. When a library dean/director mentors his or her direct reports, this also encourages and motivates those direct reports to do the same with their supervisees. In the end, it is a matter of setting the example by which the organization moves forward.

A new report on library leadership focused on talent development and digital initiatives was recently released by Ithaka S+R, and contains some interesting ideas for success (Marcum 2016). This report details ten consistent practices among successful digital organizations for encouraging and attracting digital talent into libraries, including building a comprehensive digital strategy in the organization, embracing the new rules of customer engagement, understanding global differences in how people access and use the Internet, and understanding the motivations of top talent, just to name a few.

CONCLUSION

As indicated at the beginning, I don't claim to have all the answers, and many may view my comments as plain common sense. I am always fascinated to see, however, through basic observation and through my consulting work, how often "common sense" just isn't being done by library deans/ directors, and how simple attitude and managerial changes can affect the morale and directions of the library organization. In the end (as in any politically charged situation), it is the leader who sets the tone and vision for the organization, and while legacy people and systems are often blamed for many of the challenges in academic libraries today, we as a profession have a lot to learn about the psychology and skill sets surrounding managerial and leadership situations.

REFERENCES

Curzon, Susan Carol. 2014. *What Every Library Director Should Know*. Lanham, Md.: Rowman & Littlefield.

Eden, Bradford Lee, ed. 2015–2016. Creating the 21st-Century Academic Library series. 10 vols. Lanham, Md.: Rowman & Littlefield.

———. Forthcoming. "Iterative Strategic Planning: Lessons Learned in the Trenches." In *So You Want to Be an Academic Library Director: Leadership Lessons and Critical Reflections*. Chicago: ALA Editions.

Eden, Bradford Lee, and Jody Condit Fagan, eds. 2014. *Leadership in Academic Libraries Today: Connecting Theory to Practice*. Lanham, Md.: Rowman & Littlefield.

Marcum, Deanna. 2016. *Library Leadership for the Digital Age*. New York: Ithaka S+R. Available at http://www.sr.ithaka.org/publications/library-leadership-for-the-digital-age/.

FURTHER READING

Hernon, Peter, Ronald R. Powell, and Arthur P. Young. 2003. *The Next Library Leadership: Attributes of Academic and Public Library Directors*. Westport, Conn.: Libraries Unlimited.

Matthews, Joseph R. 2005. *Strategic Planning and Management for Library Managers*. Westport, Conn.: Libraries Unlimited.

O'Connor, Steve, ed. 2015. *Library Management in Disruptive Times: Skills and Knowledge for an Uncertain Future*. London: Facet.

Smallwood, Carol, ed. 2011. *Library Management Tips That Work*. Chicago: American Library Association.

vanDuinkerken, Wyoma, and Wendi Arant Kaspar. 2015. *Leading Libraries: How to Create a Service Culture*. Chicago: ALA Editions.

vanDuinkerken, Wyoma, and Pixey Anne Mosley. 2011. *The Challenge of Library Management: Leading with Emotional Engagement*. Chicago: American Library Association.

Chapter Two

From a Transactional to Relational Model

Redefining Public Services via a Roving Pilot Program at the Georgia Tech Library

Emy Nelson Decker, Marlee Givens, and
Bruce Henson

The Georgia Institute of Technology (Georgia Tech) Library's newly instituted public service model is centered on roving staff, making use of new technology, new methods of staff training, and a new customer service ethos. Roving library staff proactively engage users as opposed to more traditional models that focus on users approaching library staff at the service desk. While roving has been offered as a supplemental service to the traditional service desk at some libraries, the Georgia Tech Library has chosen to make it the primary means by which users and library staff interact. This choice has demanded substantial, some might say radical, changes—such as the eventual removal of the public services desk—and has required a reconsideration of the ways that the library conceptualizes service as it engages its users. This chapter will provide readers with a clear case study model that sheds light on ways that librarians can lead twenty-first-century libraries in new user-focused directions. To that end, it will describe in detail the roving model at Georgia Tech. In particular, this chapter will demonstrate the importance that careful leadership has played thus far in the planning process for the rollout of the program, the strategies employed to alleviate the risk of failure, the ways that staff moved toward offering this new service model, and consideration of new methods of assessment in order to gauge impact.

LITERATURE REVIEW

Roving (also called "roaming") reference is not a new idea, but academic libraries became increasingly more interested in roving reference models in the late 1980s to mid-1990s, as they adopted online public access catalogs (OPACs) and electronic information resources. While not mentioning roving per se, Barbara Ford predicted that technological changes would necessitate a reexamination of traditional reference services and the reference desk (Ford 1986, 491–94). Boston College, perceiving a patron need for assistance with electronic resources, introduced the "reference rover," a library staff member who circulated among electronic catalog and database terminals to offer point-of-need patron service (Bregman and Mento 1992, 634). Rovers included staff from reference, circulation, and cataloging, who benefited from learning more about the library's electronic resources. Reference desk staff were relieved to refer patrons with questions about the OPAC and databases out to the rovers, freeing themselves for more complex reference transactions. In other libraries, roving seemed to be a model for increasing service to patrons who might avoid the traditional reference desk. During a pilot at Utica College, a roving reference librarian approached students and found no overlap between her roving encounters and passive reference transactions, which suggests that she was able to reach additional users and increase patron encounters through roving (Kramer 1996, 71).

The Boston and Utica studies are among several examples of roving as a supplemental service that enhances, but does not replace, the traditional reference or information desk. In some cases, the roving took place within the library, in sight of the reference desk, or in other parts of the building. At the University of Manitoba, librarians provided "a roving reference service . . . on all three floor levels" of the library (Penner 2011, 28). At Florida International University, during a pilot project, roving occurred on several floors of two library buildings. Data collected from this pilot indicated that most of the roving transactions took place in locations close to the reference desk rather than in areas without a service desk. This could be due to noise levels, as the floors with no desks were more likely to be used for quiet study, and librarians may have felt intrusive providing reference there (Askew 2015, 21–33). In other cases, librarians provided reference services outside of the library. For example, at the University of Texas at San Antonio, librarians were available in academic support areas and in student residence areas during certain hours (Del Bosque and Chapman 2007, 247–62). In some libraries, roving was part of a suite of outreach services or offered alongside virtual reference services. At the University of Northern British Columbia, roaming librarians offered services in one of three scenarios: face-to-face, by approaching a student (or being approached); via chat while roaming (with the option of face-to-face help if the chat patron was in the library); or after being paged via the chat widget to offer service at the reference desk (McCabe and MacDonald 2011).

While some studies question the traditional reference desk, very few describe programs to provide roving reference without a desk. The University of New South Wales (UNSW) Library removed its reference desk during major renovations, replacing it with a "Help Zone" near the library's entrance (Fletcher 2011). In the Help Zone, patrons encounter self-help facilities (self-checkout machines, directional kiosks, and computers for quick help), and librarians are able to provide service through computers for reference consults or in research consultation rooms. Patrons often describe the area as being "friendly," "open," or "inviting." They find the experience more comfortable without the formality of the reference desk, saying, "Normally when I go into a library the librarian behind the desk looks bored and I don't feel comfortable asking any questions." However, some patrons also regret the loss of the desk; rather than seeing the desk as a barrier to service, they were more comfortable waiting in line and understanding the visible differentiation between library staff and patrons (Fletcher 2011).

The UNSW Help Zone approach follows a customer service model seen more often in the retail world than in the traditional library. Their architect suggested that they "redefine the model of service to be less 'library-centric' and . . . more in line with current retail models, such as the Apple stores and general department stores" (Fletcher 2011). In the past, libraries have looked to the retail realm when seeking models of service quality assessment. A. Parasuraman, Valarie Zeithaml, and Leonard Berry attempted to define a conceptual model of service quality; this led to the development of an assessment instrument known as SERVQUAL, which measures the gap between customer expectations and perceptions of the service received (Parasuraman, Zeithaml, and Berry 1985, 41–50). SERVQUAL outlines five dimensions of service quality: tangibles, reliability, responsiveness, assurance, and empathy (Parasuraman, Zeithaml, and Berry 1988, 12–40). Application of SERV-QUAL in the retail environment introduced two other dimensions: problem solving and policy (Dabholkar, Thorpe, and Rentz 1996, 3). Other models have appeared since SERVQUAL was introduced, effectively summarized by Scott Baggs and Brian Kleiner in terms of their effectiveness in increasing market share, which may not be a primary consideration for a research library (Baggs and Kleiner 1996, 36–39). SERVQUAL served as the basis for the LibQUAL+ survey, which is used in many academic libraries (Association of Research Libraries Statistics and Assessment Program n.d.).

In addition to the retail world, museum models can serve as a way to offset an overt business bias by including approaches from culture-focused institutions. Leadership decisions such as these can create room to innovate and, at the same time, balance that innovation with the ongoing needs for continuity. Christina Goulding proposes that the essential "product" of a museum is the effective communication of historical information, and that interpretation of that communication depends on several factors, including the physical space but also the motivations and background of the visitor. The visitor's experience is mediated by a number of sociocultural factors, cognitive conditions, psychological orientation, and the physical environment; Goulding concludes that "the quality of the customer service encounter is therefore a question of getting the right balance between intrusion and imagination" (Goulding 2000, 274). While this study focused on self-guided visitors and did not recount interactions between visitors and museum staff or docents, it is important to note the effect of environment in the user experience as well as individual characteristics and experience that the user brings to a library service transaction. Another study looked at factors that might define expertise among docents (expertise being related to reliability and assurance, two indicators of quality customer service, and a primary reason for a user to seek assistance from library staff). Among these are knowledge, effective communication, adaptability, enthusiasm, and, notably, a sense of humor, which can put patrons at ease as well as mitigating workplace stress for the staff (Grenier 2011, 339–53).

Perceptions of service quality inform library public services both behind and away from the reference desk, and while the type of service performed may be similar in each location, patron perceptions may be different during a point-of-need roving transaction than when the patron approaches the desk. The physical space plays a large role (as seen in the differing perceptions of the UNSW library users), and the change from a transactional model to a relational model requires library staff to rely on cues other than seeing a line of patrons facing a service desk. Several studies have examined the role of nonverbal communication in library reference transactions. An early study of body movements and gestures during public service transactions in academic libraries showed the relationship between "positive" and "negative" nonverbal behaviors by library staff and perceptions of approachability and rapport by patrons (Kazlauskas 1976, 133). Positive behaviors, including eye contact, nodding to indicate listening and understanding, and cheerful facial expressions, indicated "approachability" of the library staff and increased patron interactions with staff exhibiting those behaviors. Negative behaviors, including both the lack of body movement when a patron entered the space for the reference transaction and an excess of movement (pacing or hovering) when a patron was using an item, "appeared to limit patron requests and interaction." Most notably, patrons gravitated toward staff members who were standing rather than sitting. Another study confirms some of these observations and noted that "approachable" library staff exhibited behaviors of initiation (that is, initiating the service transaction rather than waiting for the patron), availability (an open stance, or what some might call "interrupt-ability"), and proximity (close physical distance between patron and librarian) (Radford 1998, 699–718).

Lastly, several studies of roving reference focus on the tools, including iPads and other tablet devices, for completing reference transactions and for collecting assessment data. While early roving pilots occurred around OPAC and database terminals, twenty-first-century roving can take place around the library or outside the building. At the University of Manitoba, a roving project from 2005 to 2010 involved a series of devices including laptops, netbooks, Android phones, Apple iPod Touch and iPhones, and finally iPads (Penner 2011, 27–33). University of Northern British Columbia relied on iPads for their pilot (McCabe and MacDonald 2011). Florida International University also used iPads, not just for the reference transaction but for a brief user survey completed at the conclusion of the transaction (the librarian would hand the student the iPad and retrieve it after the student completed the survey) (Askew 2015, 21–33). These studies also noted some of the drawbacks of mobile reference, chiefly unreliable Wi-Fi and limited capabilities of mobile apps for catalog and database access.

PLANNING PROCESS AT GEORGIA TECH

The most important aspects of roving are to proactively seek out, engage, and assist library users (faculty, students, staff) in their scholarly work by moving throughout library spaces to provide research and reference, fulfillment (access/circulation), and technology help. As part of this customer-oriented ethos, rovers will initiate conversations with users to inquire about and assess their needs in order to determine the library resources, programs, and services that best meet their needs. To be sure, many of these tasks mirror current expectations of staff at the public services desk: to provide, both in person and virtually, frontline assistance, expertise and training with access, reference, and technology services; to assist with database and catalog searching; and to provide referrals to experts. A major difference is that new roving staff will be mobile and will provide direct customer service. Georgia Tech's service design plan for the renewed library also refers to the main public services area as the "Library Store" (Georgia Tech Library and brightspot, *Georgia Tech Library Service Design Overview* 2016). Roving staff will also be active in interpreting the science museum–like media exhibits that are planned as a key component of the Library Store.

The roving pilot program was developed based on a study with brightspot strategy consulting firm in 2013–2015. This study was connected with the "Library Next" project, which includes plans for the comprehensive renovation and renewal of the library's current buildings as well as the reimagining of the library's services and programming. The Library Store was identified as one of seven new concepts for services and spaces in the renewed library and was defined as the "face" of the library, inviting users in and engaging them in the breadth of activities, services, expertise, and collections of the library. In the store, users and service providers will work side by side at a service station or with roving staff wherever users are located. One of the overarching goals of Library Next is to "make services and expertise more visible," to connect the physical and the digital, and to make the invisible visible, including services and print and digital collections (Georgia Tech Library and brightspot, *User Research Project: Part 1* 2013).

The first roving pilot workgroup was identified in late summer 2015. During workgroup meetings, library leadership and staff began discussing the staffing and technology needs of the service. In October 2014, the Library Task Force and brightspot facilitated a prototyping workshop that provided insight for the roving pilot. In the workshop, Library Task Force members and brightspot played the roles of users and staff and tested service and space scenarios, including circulation, consultation, and referral services. Library leadership's involvement with these scenarios allowed for a more granular understanding of roving. The scenarios provided key data that continued to help inform the roving pilot. Read-throughs of the service script and a walk-through of a basic mock-up of the service space with a dress rehearsal were adapted and repeated according to what was experienced during the scenarios. Some of the workshop takeaways about workflow and referrals have been helpful in planning roving service. Workflow takeaways include: roving staff need to have backups, such as a "runner" to bring needed equipment, so they do not have to leave the user; handheld devices best serve the privacy of users in a space where others are present; the store needs more roving staff at the beginning of semesters; and roving staff need guidelines for approaching users. Referral takeaways include: the need for standard criteria and process for referrals; the preference for a "warm transfer" when possible—when a user is referred to another expert the first rover is part of the transfer process and provides information to the new expert; the need for "real-time" communication between library staff and rovers; and the important question of how rovers will identify the availability of experts to assist users immediately (Georgia Tech Library Prototyping Workshop 2014).

NEW MODEL SIGNIFICANCE

The service model in which users approach a staffed desk for help has been in place at the library for generations. The problem with this approach, however, is that it creates certain barriers between the user and the staff member. Of course, the desk itself is something of a physical barrier, but the desk also tends to influence a more transactional relationship between user and staff.

For example, a person approaches the desk, gets the assistance he or she needs, and leaves. The question arises, how might librarians break down this type of transactional exchange? One powerful way of accomplishing this is to find ways to bring staff and user side by side rather than across from each other. By working side by side, with no desk or furniture serving as a barrier, library users and staff members can have a more relational experience. By working on a query together, while looking at the same Surface tablet, for example, discovery can happen together in a way that builds community and emphasizes social interaction. In an era where libraries must continue to demonstrate their viability, the relationship between user and staff becomes an important feature.

The roving staff model at the Georgia Tech Library is a significant shift in the library's service model. There will no longer be a physical service desk with staff available to assist users who approach them. Instead, roving will provide users with a proactive, hands-on customer service model in which the user and staff member become collaborators working side by side to meet the user's needs and goals in a way that is more inviting and less hierarchical.

The potential customer service impact of the roving staff proactively engaging and assisting users in the user's workspace is tremendous as it flips the current service desk model and makes the statement that the entire library is a scholarship and research creation and learning space with expert assistance available to users "just in time" anywhere they are located. The library is committed to the roving service model and to shaping the service based on user, service, and program needs. The iterative pilots will be continually assessed by users, roving staff, and library administration. Members of the library's leadership team will use this data to adjust the program in an ongoing, "as needed" basis. Although it is still early in the process, initial expectations have begun to form. It is, for example, a working hypothesis that through such active engagement, roving staff will assume much more ownership and accountability in the library as a whole. Such investment will translate, potentially, into a greater knowledge of the interrelation of spaces, services, and resources, which in turn will increase the efficacy of their referrals to information and experts. The rovers will themselves become experts in the user's experience as they will be the staff most familiar with the library space and how users work and research there. It is also anticipated that making rovers an integral part of the library, rather than sequestering them behind a desk, will build deeper relationships with users and that this will facilitate more meaningful chances for library involvement in the research process at an early stage. The higher incidents of contact between library staff and users that roving requires will make this possible. Mobile customer service, for example, means that users who may not have in the past approached the service desk because it meant uprooting themselves from where they were working now have the opportunity to interact with library staff who are in their spaces ready to give them the help they need.

While change causes doubt among users, it is essential that in the early stages of the roving pilot, the roving pilot team builds trust among users and among staff rovers. By leading positive change and emphasizing the key components of the relational model to customer service, a positive experience with roving is expected. We anticipate that this roving model of customer service will be a positive experience for library users who are working closely with library staff. This relationship building through discovery and experiential learning may carry forward through future interactions between library users and staff.

ROVING AND NEW TECHNOLOGIES IN THE PILOT STAGE

New technologies facilitate the interactions between rovers and library users. While tablet technologies and other personal electronic devices are now a staple among the student population at the Georgia Tech Library, the roving pilot marked the first instance of customer service that necessitated the use of tablets and other small electronic devices by the staff. Early on, the library leadership team realized that for the roving model to work, it was imperative that staff members had access to, and could easily employ, portable devices that allowed them to access library resources from anywhere in the roving space. The leadership team also recognized that as the rovers would be the frontline staff for the program, it was imperative that they have a great deal of input into the tools they would be using. The members of the roving pilot program selected Microsoft Surface tablets with the Windows 10 operating system because the platform works more seamlessly with the Ex Libris Alma system that the Georgia Tech Library uses for metadata, retrieval, and fulfillment services. In order to ensure prompt check-in and checkout of library materials, the committee members chose Bluetooth barcode scanners that allow public services staff members to scan student ID cards and immediately sync the information collected with the Alma interface on their Surface tablets.

At this point in the roving pilot, the tablets and barcode scanners are individually assigned to staff participating in the roving pilot project. There will also be self-service kiosks that allow users to check out laptops. These technology-rich kiosks will provide charging, user account integration (through Alma), and user security software. The kiosks themselves will feature a touch screen with on-screen instructions and will allow users to swipe their ID cards to authenticate, charge their Alma account, and dispense a laptop. Users return laptops by simply docking them to an available slot within the kiosk. Taken together, these technologies provide users with streamlined service and help bolster the new model of customer service.

PILOT STAGE

The members of the roving pilot team met on a monthly basis from February through May 2016. These planning meetings provided opportunities to develop, design, and imagine the roving pilot and track progress toward the launch date, which took place on May 16, 2016. After the roving pilot team had convened, a special rovers' training meeting in May, prior to the launch date, taught public services staff how to make the best use of the Surface tablets and provided a crash course in retail-style body language interpretation. While the goal of roving has never been to disrupt or interrupt users, the idea is to anticipate user needs by reading subtle body language cues. An example of this might be a student looking up from a computer and looking around the room in an attempt to make eye contact with a rover. The members of the roving pilot team made special effort to not overscript the roving experience; they determined that the rovers themselves would offer the best feedback based on their direct experience interacting with the users in how to tailor the roving service at Georgia Tech Library. The leadership team let the rovers determine much of the roving experience as a means of increasing buy-in and also to encourage staff to be an integral part of the project's birth and evolution.

In order to promote the roving service, members of the Public Services Department worked to create novelty buttons that advertised the roving pilot. Members of the roving pilot were tapped to conceptualize and design the buttons, which, in turn, also help clearly mark the satchel bags worn by rovers and which hold the Surface tablets when not in use. In addition, we featured signs with the faces of roving staff members as a creative campaign to market the roving service to users entering the second, third, and fourth floors from either side of the building.

In the months leading up to the roving pilot launch, the public services team read scholarly articles about other roving public service programs in libraries and shared their takeaways from the readings. Examining the experiences of others helped prepare the team for what they might encounter. Sharing their thoughts about what they read in a group setting allowed them to proactively work to create a roving model that worked well for this environment. The readings and discussion session provided team members an opportunity to feel that they had developed a knowledge base about the subject and helped them get them excited about crafting a public services model for today's users. Projects such as these require enthusiastic staff participation so building their confidence and helping them feel competent are steps that make it more likely the pilot will succeed.

ROVING PILOT ASSESSMENT

Assessment is essential to understanding the efficacy of any service change. Since the public services model had been completely reconsidered with the roving model, a two-pronged approach to assessment was necessary to best understand the outcomes of the roving pilot. During the first few months of the roving pilot program, staff rovers were the only individuals being asked about their experience. This decision was not only practical but was also part of the library leadership signaling to staff the worth and importance of their observations. Since this model of interacting with users was entirely new to staff, and because staff had been asked to help shape the roving method of service, their input, which was collected via a ten-question Qualtrics survey, was the first priority in assessing the summer pilot program. Survey questions centered upon technology needs and issues as well as the rovers' experiences in interacting with users. Rovers reported Wi-Fi issues within certain areas of the second and third floors of the main library, and this information was then passed on to our Office of Information Technology to allow them to target and patch holes in coverage. Rovers also diligently reported verbatim comments from students who were just learning about the library's new roving program. Many of the initial comments from students were positive with remarks such as "This is really convenient," "Thank you for coming to our floors instead of having us come back downstairs to the desk," and "This [roving] is a good idea."

As would be the case with any new public service model, members of the roving pilot team anticipated some growing pains as rovers navigated an entirely new approach to working with users. Students, faculty, and staff are surveyed by librarians frequently, and we determined that it would be best to get the roving model developed during the summer, make an initial attempt at streamlining the service, and then ask our users about their experience once our rovers have developed comfort with offering this service.

FUTURE DIRECTIONS

The pilot goal is to eventually simulate as closely as possible the roving service as it will exist in the Library Store. The current pilot is offered during limited hours with half the department staff. It encompasses floors two through four of Price Gilbert and does not include the first floor, where the existing public services desk is located. Price Gilbert (four floors) and Crosland Tour (seven floors) together make up the library building. Users sometimes refer to these buildings as Library West and Library East, respectively. It is clear that the true impact of the new service cannot be assessed until there is no longer a physical public services desk and all staff are performing roving services. There is a tentative plan to physically remove the service desk in summer 2017, and the feasibility of this was assessed in January 2017, after two semesters of roving experience are complete and after a study to determine how all of the functions of the desk will be accommodated in the new service model.

A new, general position description for roving staff has been developed and vetted by library administration and is being reviewed by Georgia Tech's Human Resources Department. The position description may attract different candidates than we have previously hired as public services staff. There is a vacant position in the department and the goal is to hire an incumbent into the new position by the end of summer 2016. By the end of fall 2016, all members of the Public Services Department will have their current positions reclassified into the new roving position.

CONCLUSION

The roving pilot program at Georgia Tech has required a careful management of change and strong leadership in order to steer a new service. This case study functions as an example of the ways in which major change can be successfully navigated toward the benefit of the entire library community. Strategic service design with staff input and feedback allowed for the creation of a new service that, while completely different from the previous model, worked fluidly during the pilot program.

REFERENCES

Askew, Consuella. 2015. "A Mixed Methods Approach to Assessing Roaming Reference Services." *Evidence Based Library and Information Practice* 10 (2): 21–33.

Association of Research Libraries Statistics and Assessment Program. "LibQUAL+ Survey FAQs."https://www.libqual.org/about/about_survey/faq_survey.

Baggs, Scott C., and Brian H. Kleiner. 1996. "How to Measure Customer Service Effectively." *Managing Service Quality: An International Journal* 6 (1): 36–39.

Bregman, Adeane, and Barbara Mento. 1992. "Reference Roving at Boston College: Point of Use Assistance to Electronic Resource Users Reduces Stress." *College & Research Libraries News* 53: 634–35.

Dabholkar, Pratibha A., Dayle I. Thorpe, and Joseph O. Rentz. 1996. "A Measure of Service Quality for Retail Stores: Scale Development and Validation." *Journal of the Academy of Marketing Science* 24 (1): 3.

Del Bosque, Darcy, and Kimberly Chapman. 2007. "Your Place or Mine? Face-to-Face Reference Services across Campus." *New Library World* 108 (5/6): 247–62.

Fletcher, Jane. 2011. "Breaking Down the Barriers—the No Desk Academic Library." Paper presented at the Effect of Technologies on Library Design: Building the 21st Century Library, Atlanta, Ga., August 10–11.

Ford, Barbara J. 1986. "Reference beyond (and without) the Reference Desk." *College & Research Libraries* 47 (5): 491–94.

Georgia Tech Library and brightspot. 2014. *Georgia Tech Library Service Design Overview.* http://www.library.gatech.edu/about/docs/GT-Library-Service-Design-Overview.pdf.

———. 2014. *Prototyping Workshop.*

———. 2016. *User Research Project: Part 1: Research Report & Playbook.* http://www.library.gatech.edu/about/docs/part1.pdf.

Goulding, Christina. 2000. "The Museum Environment and the Visitor Experience." *European Journal of Marketing* 34 (3/4): 261–78.

Grenier, Robin S. 2011. "Taking the Lead: A Qualitative Study of Expert Docent Characteristics." *Museum Management and Curatorship* 26 (4): 339–53.

Kazlauskas, Edward. 1976. "An Exploratory Study: A Kinesic Analysis of Academic Library Public Service Points." *Journal of Academic Librarianship* 2 (3): 130–34.

Kramer, Eileen H. 1996. "Why Roving Reference: A Case Study in a Small Academic Library." *Reference Services Review* 24 (3): 67–80.

McCabe, Kealin M, and James R. W. MacDonald. 2011. "Roaming Reference: Reinvigorating Reference through Point of Need Service." *Partnership: The Canadian Journal of Library and Information Practice and Research* 6 (2).

Parasuraman, A., Valarie A. Zeithaml, and Leonard L. Berry. 1985. "A Conceptual Model of Service Quality and Its Implications for Future Research." *Journal of Marketing* 49 (4): 41–50.

———. 1988. "SERVQUAL: A Multiple-Item Scale for Measuring Consumer Perceptions of Service Quality." *Journal of Retailing* 64 (1): 12–40.

Penner, Katherine. 2011. "Mobile Technologies and Roving Reference." *Public Services Quarterly* 7 (1–2): 27–33.

Radford, Marie L. 1998. "Approach or Avoidance? The Role of Nonverbal Communication in the Academic Library User's Decision to Initiate a Reference Encounter." *Library Trends* 46 (4): 699–718.

Chapter Three

Leading Changes in Library as an Architect of Technology Infrastructure

Hong Ma

Systems librarians play the role of intermediary between technology and its implementation in libraries (Breeding 2014). In earlier times, the title "systems librarian" was designated for the person responsible for the integrated library system (ILS). Today, the intermediary role persists, but systems librarians can no longer tie their expertise only to the ILS. Instead, the systems librarian serves as an information systems architect who is familiar with a much wider scope of technologies. There are different titles and levels of administrative authority associated with the position depending on the organizational structure (Breeding 2014). The titles used are not only systems librarian but also digital/web services librarian, head of library systems, director or coordinator of library information technology, chief technology officer (CTO), chief information officer (CIO), and assistant/associate university librarian for technology. The common thing is that the individual who plays a role as information technology architect needs to keep up a broad view of technology and how it can benefit the library, taking a lead on reshaping the library technology infrastructure to ensure it meets strategic priorities and operational requirements. To take on this role, systems librarians face the challenge of keeping up to date with their knowledge and skill sets in technology, as well as in the areas of leadership, project management, and communications.

This chapter will focus on how systems librarians can evolve from providing operational support of library systems to serving as architects of the library's technology infrastructure. It will also highlight how they can lean into the leadership role necessary to implement technological change that will meet users' increasing expectations. It will then describe a case study showing how one systems librarian—the "head of library systems" at Loyola University Chicago Libraries—made efforts to evolve and successfully transformed her role to that of an architect leading her library in the migration to a next-generation library automation system and implementation of a new discovery tool.

THE TECHNOLOGY REVOLUTION IN HIGHER EDUCATION

Higher education has been experiencing a dramatic revolution in the last decade. As Stephen J. Laster (2012) states, "These are interesting times for higher education and its supporting technologist. Never before has higher education been more expensive, and never before has technology been so well positioned to profoundly impact the future of teaching, learning, and organizational sustainability." Changes are happening in scholarly communications practices. Technology brings new ways to disseminate knowledge and information and offers better ways to perform scholarly work. It revolutionized how knowledge is communicated (Laster 2012).

Distance learning brings an area of enormous potential for higher education systems around the world that are struggling to meet the needs of growing and changing student populations (Rogers 2000). Collaborative research trends are represented as interdisciplinary, computer intensive, and taking place in an increasingly digital environment. Higher education is moving to a blended learning environment, a learning environment that combines face-to-face instruction with technology-mediated instruction (Graham and Dziuban 2008). Academic workforces are being restructured, while instructional technologies have been adopted for teaching and learning. The development of technology-enhanced learning is accelerating exponentially. Artificial intelligence makes it possible to personalize the online classroom, even when course content is being distributed to a mass audience (DeMillo and Young 2015). Personalized learning and adaptive learning have become popular in higher education. Virtual and physical spaces coexist. Innovations like massive open online courses (MOOCs), through which simple course content can be replicated and distributed to anyone with an Internet connection, change the traditional path of college education.

Clifford Lynch (2000, 60) emphasizes, "Information technology has profoundly changed all aspects of higher education and scholarship, and these changes continue to unfold today. Innovation and transformation for academic libraries take place within this broader context."

THE CHANGING ROLES OF ACADEMIC LIBRARIES

The shift to electronic content is one of the most obvious things that has changed in the last decade for academic libraries, fundamentally changing how information is accessed and used. Libraries buy fewer physical items and put fewer used items into storage, which allows them to rethink their physical spaces and services. At the same time, pedagogical practices have changed, as demonstrated by an increased emphasis on collaborative learning and projects. Innovative libraries have become as important as the classroom or the laboratory as places where engaged learning takes place. Libraries have changed from being quiet repositories of books to active community centers "filled" with both physical and digital materials (Hibel 2015). Libraries started renovating spaces to meet new patron needs. Information commons/learning commons have become popular on college campuses. With new technologies such as 3D printers, makerspaces also have become an integral part of many libraries' learning spaces. As Kathryn Zickuhr, Lee Rainie, and Kristen Purcell (2013) state, "Libraries are really transforming themselves into technology hubs."

Clifford Lynch (2000, 66) states, "Library collections have transformed into network services and have become deeply integrated into campus information services." During the past decade, a period that Lynch defines as the "automation period," libraries were focused on the implementation and management of technology. Now libraries have entered a completely new phase that he calls the "transformation period." As Lynch emphasizes, "Libraries now must turn their attention to define their mission and activities in relationship to their transforming context—the information technology revolution in teaching, learning and research" (Lynch 2000). Obviously transformation will be much harder than automation.

A new generation is joining universities with new expectations for online teaching, blended learning and digitally supported research. These faculty and students desire access to information and services on a 24/7 basis, from any location. They are not only information consumers but also data contributors. All of these factors are affecting and changing the context of academic libraries.

The core mission of academic libraries still remains one of collecting content, providing access to that content, and storing it for the future; however, the way that libraries operate is changing. Academic libraries started developing and implementing new strategic planning processes to redefine their roles for this new higher education environment. New focuses for libraries include: digitizing and providing access to local unique collections; planning for long-term preservation of these unique collections; building institutional repositories to support scholarly communications; building partnerships on and off campus to develop new programs such as data management services; and collaborating with campus IT units to create technologically advanced learning spaces. It is essential to articulate the library's value to the academic community by finding new ways to get involved and ensure the library's contribution to institutional effectiveness.

There are many visions of how academic libraries will continue to evolve. In 2012, the Association of Research Libraries (ARL) started developing strategic thinking and design with a talk by John Seely Brown titled "Changing How We Think about and Lead Change" (Brown 2012), and then followed up with a series of developing processes to build a "system of action" to shape the future of research libraries. A report with a detailed description of this innovative process and framework was released in February 2014 (Baughman et al. 2014). The report states the vision as follows: "In 2033, the research library will have shifted from its role as a knowledge service provider within the university to become a collaborative partner within a rich and diverse learning and research ecosystem" (Baughman et al. 2014). The dean of Brigham Young University (BYU), Dr. Paustenbaugh, was asked how she envisioned libraries evolving. She replied: "While I think the library as place will continue to have relevance and that we will continue to license content that cannot be acquired in any other way, the main contribution of the library will be as an integral collaborative partner in the teaching, learning, and research processes" (Hibel 2015).

HOW SYSTEMS LIBRARIANS ARE EVOLVING FROM TECHNICAL EXPERTS TO ARCHITECTS OF TECHNOLOGY INFRASTRUCTURE

As mentioned in the introduction section, systems librarians arose from the need for experts to lead the implementation and management of technology at the library. This job, with a variety of titles and descriptions, was created primarily for managing library integrated systems (ILS). Along with libraries' technological transformation, the systems librarian's role has been evolving and transforming from one of ILS manager to systems architect. These librarians no longer work behind the curtain and wait for the support requests arriving from other library units. Given the context of fast-paced technological developments, the challenge academic libraries are facing is to evaluate and decide which technologies will do the most to enhance library services. This brings opportunities for a systems librarian to fit into the role of architect quite naturally. Marshall Breeding (2014) articulates that while "'Systems librarian' may not be used quite as much as the earlier days of library automation, libraries must continue to see the need for an intermediary architect able to optimally shape the library's technical infrastructure."

A systems librarian first needs to be someone who has a solid understanding about information technology and how it would impact the library, but he or she also needs to be library savvy. As Marshall (2014) emphasizes again, "One cannot effectively manage technology for an organization without understanding its strategic purpose and its daily operational tasks." Librarians need to use technology in almost every aspect of their job on a daily basis, so the spectrum of technologies and systems with which the systems librarian has to be fluent has broadened. Fortunately, new trends in cloud computing and software as a service (SaaS) reduce the low-level infrastructure needs for libraries, allowing systems librarians to focus on higher-level, more library-specific functions and user-centered services.

Systems librarians can play a leadership role in building and shaping the library's technical environment by acting as an architect through a variety of processes. Major library technologies, such as next-generation library management systems and discovery tools, are selected through formal evaluation and selection processes with a wide range of library departments and personnel involved. Constructing the technology environment is complex and cannot be done by a single person, but the systems librarian should play an essential leadership role, influencing and leading these processes to ensure the best choices are being made (Breeding 2014).

Case Study: Systems Librarian as an Architect of Library Technology

In 2014, Loyola University Chicago Libraries began the process of developing a new three-year (2014–2017) strategic plan. The head of library systems, a systems librarian, was part of the management team who developed the strategic goals. The first goal was identified as follows: "The University Libraries will increase comprehensive and convenient access to local and worldwide scholarly information for the Loyola community" (University Libraries Loyola University Chicago 2014). The legacy ILS coupled with an online public access catalog (OPAC) was no longer adequate for managing a variety of different formats of information resources. To make up for the absence of necessary functions for electronic resources and local digital assets in ILS, a series of ancillary products such as a link resolver, an electronic resource management (ERM) system, a digital asset management (DAM) system, and a web-scale discovery service was implemented. It has been challenging to maintain all these silos in such a nonintegrated environment. Along with the first goal, a strategy was built to improve ease of discovery and access to information in all formats by reinventing the information infrastructure, moving away from system silos to a unified management platform.

A process to select and implement a next-generation ILS was established. Marshall Breeding named what was well known as next-generation ILS a "library services platform" (LSP) (Breeding 2011). An LSP aims to provide a comprehensive approach to managing library collections, handling diverse print and electronic formats in unified workflow to simplify library operations. Most LSPs are built on service-oriented architecture (SOA), and are deployed through cloud-based infrastructures and provide web-based interfaces. Most LSP vendors provide software as a service (SaaS). The goal was to evaluate and select the right product to improve the internal library workflow as well as to provide the Loyola community with an intuitive and sophisticated tool to discover and gain access to scholarly resources and library collections of increasing complexity, depth, and breadth. The Next-Generation ILS Exploratory Committee and subcommittees were appointed by the dean of libraries in January 2014. The head of library systems was appointed as the chair of the committee. Committee and subcommittee members included people from a variety of library departments, as well as representatives from campus IT. The chair started a collaborative selection process and educated all library staff with an overview of the new technology-related terms and concepts such as cloud computing, SOA, SaaS, and so forth. Then she established a collaborative process to develop the formal RFP (request for proposal), coordinated vendor webinars and demonstrations, while encouraging and ensuring full library staff participation for each candidate system. In addition to communicating with vendors, the committee also interviewed peer institutions who recently implemented LSPs. In July 2014, the committee delivered a report to library administration that summarized the pros and cons for each system and included their recommendation for the selection of Ex Libris's Alma as a next-generation library resources management system, and Ex Libris's Primo as the discovery tool. After a couple of follow-up discussions between the committee and library administration, a final decision to choose Alma/Primo was made in October 2014, with the contract to purchase a single instance of the system signed in December 2014.

After the contract was signed, a collaborative implementation process was immediately established. The head of library systems continued to chair the implementation team and served as the project manager. She carried forward the collaborative culture developed during the vendor selection process. After looking closely at a couple of other libraries' experiences, an implementation team was built, consisting of a series of working groups (Access Services, Acquisition and Resource Management, ERM, Primo/Discovery, and Systems) to focus on migration and implementation details for each functional area and an executive group to focus on policy, vision, planning, communications, and decision making. In the middle of implementation, due to the complexity of the electronic resources and the libraries' multicampus context, she identified that more in-depth and frequent collaborations were needed among campuses as well as among the public services, technical services, and systems staff members. Another cross-departmental group called "Electronic Resources Access and Troubleshooting Group" was formed to investigate best practices for managing electronic resources to provide a better user discovery experience.

The Alma/Primo implementation project was kicked off in January 2015 when the Ex Libris team came on-site and provided an overview of the project to all library staff. Weekly project calls started after the kickoff. The leads of each working group took on detailed implementation tasks and the majority of the decision making was distributed to the functional working groups.

As project manager, the head of library systems oversaw the project as a whole, ensuring all communications between the institution and Ex Libris, coordinating activities, and communicating with all parties, keeping the library administration and library staff who were not participating in the implementation process updated. She also served as lead for the Systems working group in charge of core technical pieces of migration tasks.

The well-developed implementation structure, along with the collaborative and decentralized management model, kept things moving in an efficient way. However, there were also unexpected challenges. For example, there are resources shared by all campuses, as well as resources limited to health sciences users only. The Health Sciences Library uses a separate EZproxy server for authentication of the resources available to its users. The built-in electronic resource management solution in Alma (single-institution instance) requires all patrons be loaded into predefined network groups to gain access to specific licensed resources. Not all health sciences patrons could be loaded into Alma. Their staff information system was not accessible because the hospital system is owned by a different corporate entity. In order to resolve the issue, the systems librarian had to coordinate all efforts, reaching out to other institutions for advice, consulting with experts at Ex Libris, and researching the structure of Alma and Primo. Eventually, they identified an acceptable solution for all campuses by double activating the shared resources and utilizing a public note to create a standard access message for users. The process of dealing with this unexpected challenge improved the relationship and collaboration among campuses, even though it put the library behind its initially agreed-upon timeline with Ex Libris.

For the implementation of Primo, a formal usability testing process was established by the lead of the Primo working group, the digital services librarian, who is a direct report to the head of library systems. The process continued through the system's go-live. The results of usability testing drove changes and customizations to Primo directly. The group created two versions of the interface with a different set of customizations and labeling, tested both with a group of students, and then picked the most popular options for an additional test before opening the interface as a public beta in

June of 2015. They left the beta version of Primo up for a month to gather further users' feedback for further site revisions before launching the live site on July 23, 2015.

After the successful implementation of a next-generation library services platform with its two major components—resource management and re-source discovery—a solid technological foundation has been built for the Loyola University Chicago Libraries. The head of library systems and the digital services librarian continue to promote the culture of collaboration and data-driven principles for enhancing both the library services platform and the library's web presence. The head of library systems reshaped the Alma/Primo implementation team as an ongoing Alma/Primo committee and con-tinues to provide leadership to that team. A data-driven decision-making process has been established as one of its guiding principles. The digital services librarian continues to lead the Primo working group and also works closely with the web team, which is also chaired by her. She has established a formal methodology for usability testing and uses the results from testing to guide agile development processes. The web team also contributes data gath-ered through a variety of tools (e.g., Google Analytics) for the libraries' evidence-based decision making.

The Systems Department is fairly small, including the head of library systems, the digital services librarian, the server administrator, and a couple of student workers. So it is crucial to make best use of resources and seek ways to collaborate with library committees or other campus partners. A couple of continuing enhancement and integration projects have been iden-tified by the Systems Department that demonstrate the breadth of the role of today's systems librarians. In the summer of 2016, the head of library sys-tems reached out to campus IT services and started the conversation of im-plementing single sign-on between Primo, ILLiad, and the library's EZproxy server by setting up SAML (security assertion markup language) with Shib-boleth. The integration between Alma and the campus financial system has been identified and planned. Internally, the Systems Department worked with special collections units to enhance the discoverability of unique Loyola collections. A Digital Preservation Committee (DPC) was formed to address the long-term goals for digital preservation. This group also has been led by the digital services librarian. The DPC has been working on evaluating digi-tal preservation systems, and made a recommendation for choosing a system called Preservica that will be used as tool for digital preservation. The Sys-tems Department continues to maintain other library systems such as Con-tentDM, eCommons, Omeka, and so forth. The Systems Department played an essential role in building new partnerships with other campus units out-side of the library. The head of library systems and the digital services librarian sit in the Academic Technology Committee (ATC) to contribute ideas about how to get faculty buy-in for adopting new technologies to enhance teaching and learning. Recently, some new partnerships with other campus units were established. For example, the Center for Textual Studies initialized a Digital Humanities Steering (DHS) Committee. A couple of library staff people, including the digital services librarian, were invited to join the committee, which works with faculty members on digital humanities projects.

The head of library systems and the digital services librarian pay close attention to new technology trends and their impact on libraries through professional publications and conferences. They both maintain a strong record of service to the profession as well as contributing to professional research and publications. They have active roles in key professional organizations such as the Library Information Technology Association (LITA). Being active in professional development and services helps them to stay relevant and aware of forthcoming technology trends and to make judgements about the application and impact of these technology trends.

CONCLUSION

In today's information technology environment, assessment has become essential for decision making on what services should be offered and what services need to be retired in academic libraries. While librarians are excited about evidence-based decision making, more challenges are on the way. On one hand, they are making efforts to capture users' behavior across library platforms; on the other hand, they have to struggle to balance how they can continue to protect users' privacy in this data-driven environment.

To build an efficient and effective library technology infrastructure, the most challenging situation systems librarians face is how to integrate many different technology pieces together, some inherited from the past, some imposed externally, some developed in-house, some upgraded recently through a library-wide process. It is essential to have different applications work together, communicating data as needed and avoiding redundancy of work. It is also crucial for the library technology applications to communicate well with other applications on campus to support learning, teaching, and researching activities. The expertise of systems librarians continues to provide opportunities for them to explore new technologies and lean into leadership roles where their improvement of technology infrastructure can support the library's strategic goals and daily operations. As innovation continues, new skill sets beyond those of the type of leadership, communications, and project management that are discussed in this chapter may be required. Systems librarians need to be agile enough to be able to adopt new knowledge as they continue to serve in the intersection between technology and libraries.

REFERENCES

Baughman, Sue, David Consiglio, Lee Anne George, Susan Gibbons, David Gift, Kaylyn Groves, Tom Hickerson, et al. 2014. *Report of the Association of Research Libraries Strategic Thinking and Design Initiative.* Association of Research Libraries. http://www.arl.org/ storage/documents/publications/strategic-thinking-design-full-report-aug2014.pdf.

Breeding, Marshall. 2011. "The Systems Librarian: A Cloudy Forecast for Libraries." *Computers in Libraries* 31 (7): 32–34.

———. 2014. "Shape Up Your Skills and Shake Up Your Library." *Computers in Libraries* 34 (1): 17–19.

Brown, John Seely. 2012. "Changing How We Think about and Lead Change." Paper presented at the ARL Fall Forum, Arlington, Va., October 12. http://www.arl.org/storage/ documents/publications/ff12-brown.pdf.

DeMillo, Richard A., and Andrew J. Young. 2015. *Revolution in Higher Education: How a Small Band of Innovators Will Make College Accessible and Affordable.* Cambridge, Mass.: MIT Press.

Graham, Charles R., and Charles Dziuban. 2008. "Blended Learning Environments." In *Handbook of Research on Educational Communications and Technology,* edited by Michael J. Spector, 269–76. New York: Erlbaum.

Hibel, Andrew. 2015. "The Changing Roles of Academic and Research Libraries." Interview with Jennifer Paustenbaugh in Higher Ed Careers. https://www.higheredjobs.com/ higheredcareers/interviews.cfm?ID=632.https://www.higheredjobs.com/higheredcareers/ interviews.cfm?ID=632.

Laster, Stephen J. 2012. "Rethinking Higher Education Technology." *EDUCAUSE Review* 47 (3): 62–63.

Lynch, Clifford. 2000. "From Automation to Transformation: Forty Years of Libraries and Information Technology in Higher Education." *EDUCAUSE Review* 35 (1): 60–68.

Rogers, Donna L. 2000. "A Paradigm Shift: Technology Integration for Higher Education in the New Millennium." *Educational Technology Review* 13 (Spring/Summer): 19–27.

University Libraries Loyola University of Chicago Strategic Plan, July 2014–June 2017. 2014.

Zickuhr, Kathryn, Lee Rainie, and Kristen Purcell. 2013. *Library Services in the Digital Age.* Pew Internet & American Life Project, January 22. http://libraries.pewinternet.org/files/ legacy-pdf/PIP_Library%20services_Report.pdf.

FURTHER READING

Brown, Malcolm. 2016. "The Future of Learning Environments in Higher Education: EDUCAUSE Learning Initiative Examines the NGDLE in Spring Focus Session." *EDUCAUSE Review: Transforming Higher Ed,* April 8. http://er.educause.edu/blogs/2016/4/the-future-of-learning-environments-in-higher-education.

Dobbin, Gregory. 2016. "Six Ways to Support Personalized Learning." *EDUCAUSE Review,* April 4. http://er.educause.edu/articles/2016/4/six-ways-to-support-personalized-learning.

Part II

Entrepreneurship

Chapter Four

The Entrepreneurial Spirit Lives in Librarians

Mary G. Scanlon and Michael A. Crumpton

LEADING INNOVATION

Historically and currently, libraries have encouraged and enabled entrepreneurial activities for patrons across a wide spectrum of interests. Common ways in which libraries support entrepreneurs include business-related resources, guidance from business librarians, enhanced technology access, and space in which to meet, conduct research, and work (Wapner 2016). Librarians often share their patrons' dreams of creating new knowledge or improving their situations. This support occurs in libraries of all types: university, community college, and public libraries. Most recently, it's apparent in the growth of "makerspaces" supplied by libraries to encourage creative thinking.

John Burke, from Miami University Middletown, shared a concise view of makerspaces at the 2014 Conference for Entrepreneurial Librarians and explained why this type of innovation belongs in libraries. Using assessment data to support his views, Burke made the argument that by providing space and support to "maker" activities, this reinforces the libraries' mission to educate and provide each library community the means to be innovative and creative.

As libraries try to find their way in a changing world, new and innovative ways of thinking are required to continue providing value to their patrons and their communities. In addition, it's important that they communicate their value to their funding sources, be they institutional or governmental, to justify financial investment in them. Academic libraries in particular must compete with technological developments that often mislead students and faculty into believing there's no need to come to a physical building to seek information. As expectations change for what the library experience means to individuals personally, librarians must become entrepreneurial themselves in order to better align with users' needs. In defining this new model of service, influenced by technology and dynamic cultural change, perhaps we can consider ourselves in the relationship business (Mathews 2014, 16–24), which also leads to new ways of connecting and interacting with stakeholders.

This cultural significance was demonstrated by a second webinar held by the team of conference planners in conjunction with ALA's Library Leadership, Administration and Management division. This webinar presented three examples of how libraries were embracing societal values to promote social entrepreneurship for collaborative and beneficial purposes, which helps develop relationships to create ongoing innovative endeavors ("Social Entrepreneurship: Digitizing our Cultural History" 2012).

Librarians have served and supported users and their entrepreneurial activities for many years but are just now recognizing their own entrepreneurial spirit and the impact that can have. Recognizing the traits of entrepreneurial thinking is not always obvious, as innovation is considered to be something self-developed, rather than taught (Ehrlichman 2016). Being passionate, optimistic, willing to take risks, and questioning conventional methods are all considered traits not traditionally embedded in the profession. It takes leadership and the ability to motivate and inspire to drive others toward thinking as entrepreneurs and influencing the organization positively (Pierce 2008).

In a presentation presented at the 2014 Conference for Entrepreneurial Librarians, Amanda Binder and Lareese Hall discussed an idea to encourage innovation and creativity, within their library staffs; they called it CoP, or communities of practice, which was an initiative of their Professional Activities Committee. They encouraged their staffs by supporting a variety of collaborative activities such as: writing groups, research workgroups, peer-mentoring activities, and professional advancement discussions. They compared this type of business model adapted by successful companies to fostering an entrepreneurial experience for librarians.

The gaming industry provides an example of dynamic methods of changing how problems are solved, conflicts are resolved, and creativity is used to develop new ideas. As gaming moves from an entertainment-driven focus into a greater use for training and learning, it also provides the opportunity to increase an individual's ability to creatively solve problems (Mendez and Del Moral 2015, 211–18). Simply put, gamers must develop new solutions at each run of the game in order to beat or get past the previous termination point. This encourages experimentation and creative risk taking in order to advance.

Librarians are learning that experimentation and risk taking are needed to break out of old methods and to catch up with emerging trends. Being willing to look at operations and services from a critical point of view can lead to new methods and influence the organization's culture to do the same (Bloom 2016, 12–13). It's important to recognize that change is constant but how individuals and organizations approach change is varied and not always successful. Change within the profession is benchmarked in Miriam Drake's update to her 1993 paper related to technological change (Drake 2000, 53–59). Drake feels that in the so-called information age the increasing use of technology has become the driving force in the way people work, learn, and play. She demonstrates that change can and will continue to occur, but it is still possible to sustain the values of librarianship and commitment to intellectual freedom.

Librarians need to recognize and embrace characteristics that nurture the entrepreneurial spirit. While entrepreneurial education is primarily focused on business and manufacturing concerns, learning how to convert individual and collective experiences into something new is a basic component of entrepreneurialism that librarians can and should pursue ("Nurturing the Entrepreneurial Spirit" n.d.). These are the characteristics of leadership and include good communication, emotional intelligence, and a willingness to challenge the status quo. Collaboration is also important for supporting entrepreneurial endeavors as has been demonstrated by a conference devoted to entrepreneurial librarians that will be described later in this chapter (Scanlon and Crumpton 2011, 16–27). In this case, collaboration began a series of collaborative activities that have expanded the entrepreneurial mind-set within libraries, resulting in a series of presentations and publications that support the entrepreneurial spirit.

In 2015, Laura Saunders published a study related to underrecognized areas of strategic planning (Saunders 2015, 285–91). She concludes that, in many cases, academic libraries are still reacting to long-range resource allocation planning without being strategic about other options. This indicates a need for more innovative leadership that would explore new models or options for resource allocation and service requests. Her report also suggests that emerging trends, which potentially lead libraries away from traditional forms of operation, are being ignored in favor of prioritization of resources that may not align with missions and goals.

Leadership becomes the key ingredient in establishing an entrepreneurial mind-set by allowing individual innovation to solve problems of a strategic nature. To be innovative is to not follow a model of narrowly defined metrics, but to look for diverse and inclusive ways to broaden community, provide open access to information, and develop a community of influence (Walter and Lankes 2015, 854–58). Critical assessment of trends matched to available resources can produce unpopular conclusions, and the effective leader will help others in the organization see the benefit of the innovation. Considering what might happen, could occur, or is likely to develop by following a particular path is also a visionary method for determining how decisions can be made strategically.

Visionary leaders share common traits that are in large part attributed to emotional intelligence (Goleman, Boyatzis, and McKee 2013). The characteristics of emotional intelligence, packaged as strength in self-confidence, self-awareness, and empathy, describe a visionary leader with a strong sense of purpose who can lead others toward a goal. In doing so, transparency is a major competency that leaders must demonstrate to show others there is nothing to hide.

Leaders motivate others in order to move an issue forward. What motivates librarians to be innovative or entrepreneurial? Steven Bell identifies five qualities or characteristics that leaders should look for in individuals in order to help motivate and nurture that spirit of innovation (Bell 2009, 18–19). They are: opportunistic, creative, persistent, risk taking, and being able to connect the dots. Persons with these characteristics are more likely to pursue creative ideas for solving problems and finding ways to add value in an increasingly competitive environment. Bell likens these abilities to those of well-known entrepreneurs, but also to librarians who have demonstrated new and innovative skills within our profession.

Within the organization, leaders must develop and possess a set of values from which they operate (Crumpton 2015). Values that encourage an entrepreneurial spirit include:

- Innovation and creativity
- Accountability and excellence in service and programming
- A culture of diversity and inclusion
- Communication that empowers and fosters openness
- Culture of sustainability
- Collaboration and teamwork
- Atmosphere of continual learning

These values can fuel leadership's success in moving innovative agendas forward.

The need for broader entrepreneurial thinking is addressed from other sources, such as the Kauffman Foundation and its report on entrepreneurship in higher education. This report became the impetus for these authors' initial efforts on celebrating entrepreneurship in libraries because of their description of a comprehensive educational climate that is transformative, creative, and innovative (Bazirjian 2009, 16–17). This report correlated with librarians who need to be innovative in seeking resources, programming challenges to keep patrons informed, and learning how to keep up with technology and maintain relevance. Librarians are part of this transformative climate because of our work serving an increasingly complex and dynamic set of information needs for others and having a broad sense of social responsibility as good stewards of information. Proactive leadership can help motivate librarians to adopt skills and characteristics that embrace a spirit of innovation and develop innovations that can add value and enhance our professional mantra.

Change is occurring rapidly and will continue at a fast pace in the future, which creates the scenario of a convergence of user needs, libraries' capabilities, and competitive options, or sometimes referred to as the sweet spot (Hernon and Matthews 2013). Librarians by training are expected to support constituent needs with their services and resources, in order to build community and develop a society for continued knowledge creation. Learning how to direct the entrepreneurial spirit into attributes that help librarians help themselves is a necessary step in remaining vital and competitive for the future. Library leaders must embrace entrepreneurial characteristics by motivating others, demonstrating a diverse point of view, and being inclusive of all ideas and possibilities.

THE ENTREPRENEURIAL ORGANIZATION

Librarians are more likely to behave entrepreneurially when they work in organizations that foster entrepreneurship. Once a leader has recognized the advantages of cultivating such an organization, he or she might consider how to develop these traits in their library (3 Amigas NCLA Presentation on Entrepreneurship, Krautter, Lock, and Scanlon 2015).

According to Jeffrey Cornwall and Baron Perlman:

> Culture is an organization's basic beliefs and assumptions about what the organization is all about, how its members should behave, and how it defines itself in relation to its external environment. A culture is an organization's reality, and culture shapes all that goes on within an organization. A culture is reflected in an organization's philosophies, rules, norms, values, climate, symbols, heroes, and almost everything its members do. (Cornwall and Perlman 1990, 66)

Lawrence James et al. (2007, 21) describe culture as "the normative beliefs (i.e., system values) and shared behavioral expectations (i.e., system norms) in an organization." James Sarros, Brian Cooper, and Joseph Santora (2008, 145–58) assert that upper-echelon leaders establish organizational culture and have the ability to transform it.

Thus, developing an entrepreneurial culture in one's library is the first step in developing these thought patterns, approaches, and behaviors among librarians and library staff. It's easy to find lists of the characteristics of entrepreneurial organizational culture. Cornwall and Perlman (1990), Sarros, Cooper, and Santora (2008), and Stephanie Jones (2014) provide their key characteristics. After reading through the literature, Mary Krautter, Mary Beth Lock, and Mary G. Scanlon (2015) distilled them down to three that remained constant across many models: communication, empowerment, and rewards.

Krautter, Lock, and Scanlon have been part of the committee that has been organizing the Conference for Entrepreneurial Librarians since 2008. Their book *The Entrepreneurial Librarian* (Krautter, Lock, and Scanlon 2013) grew out of the conference and led to two speaking opportunities: an invitation to present a workshop and panel discussion at the annual conference for the Arabian Gulf States section of the Special Libraries Association in 2015, and a presentation at the North Carolina Libraries Association, also in 2015. For each characteristic they provide practical advice from both top-down and bottom-up approaches for implementing these characteristics in an organization.

Communication begins with a clear statement of the organization's mission statement. All innovation should be in direct service to the mission and the library's patrons. The mission and values must be well known and thoroughly infused into the organization to ensure that everyone in the organization understands their purpose and how their position and job responsibilities serve them. Creativity must serve this master. In other words, decision making, innovation, and problem solving should be aligned with the organization's mission and values.

Once the mission is ingrained in the organization's psyche, the leader who is transforming her organization into an entrepreneurial one will communicate the pressures on the organization; these might be financial, political, demographic, or technological. Libraries must respond to changes from many forces, both internal and external. Financial constraints are a constant and libraries must adapt to tight budgets and rising costs. Changes in patron demographics, usage patterns and trends, needs and wants are always shifting. Does it need to be said that technology is always changing? Librarians already know that they must keep pace with the new opportunities presented by evolving technology. These should be shared with the organization so people can understand why library operations and staffing patterns are being revised. Transparency about pressures facing the organization as well as the decision-making process creates a sense of openness that builds trust. In addition, people are more likely to embrace change when they understand the need for it.

The leader of an entrepreneurial organization will exhibit the following behaviors according to Krautter, Lock, and Scanlon (2013):

- Maintain an open-door policy
- Exhibit transparency in decision making
- Allow dissension, not derailment

• Provide a safe place for risk takers

Colleagues need to feel heard and respected, and an open-door policy will support this. They should feel safe bringing new ideas to their supervisor or leader. Such an atmosphere will encourage colleagues to bring forth more ideas.

Transparency in decision making creates a sense that they all know what's going on and why they're doing what they're doing. It fosters an atmosphere of inclusion, mutual respect, and trust, which are important to an entrepreneurial culture. When they all know the mission, the challenges, and the means by which they're moving forward, colleagues are more likely to feel that they have a stake in the organization's future and its success.

Bottom-up communication is equally important in this environment. In organizations in which an entrepreneurial culture is being fostered, colleagues at any level are potential sources of ideas. Innovation and creativity should be encouraged, and supervisors must maintain an open door and an open mind. Supervisors should listen carefully to colleagues' ideas and encourage idea development. Yes, some ideas are better than others and some are more expensive or risky to implement, but supervisors should treat each person's idea with respect regardless. Colleagues can be encouraged to move forward with their ideas by doing research into the costs, developing a timeline to implementation, and studying the patron group that will benefit from it or the nature of the changes to internal operations. These pieces of information will help the organization determine if the idea should be pursued, if additional resources should be invested in its development, and whether a pilot project should be launched. If the organization decides to further develop it, it will become important to give colleagues the time and mental space to work on such project, rather than expecting them to add the project's management to their existing responsibilities.

Open channels of communication do not guarantee that everyone will agree with the plan or embrace it wholeheartedly. Change is more difficult for some than for others, and even when colleagues agree on a general direction there can be concerns and differences of opinion on the exact plan for moving forward. Dissenting opinions should be heard and entertained. While the perils of groupthink are well known and documented (Bowie 2013, 183–205), naysayers should not be allowed to derail a good idea.

Risk taking is absolutely necessary in an entrepreneurial organization. Every time an organization tries a new way of doing something there is a risk that it may not turn out exactly as planned. This should be understood and tolerated in an entrepreneurial organization. Punishing failure will discourage colleagues from contributing their ideas. Instead of punishing disappointments, examine them. Learn from them. What didn't work out and why not? Can the idea be modified and tried again? This is the Google model:

launch it, assess it, and fix it. Everything is in beta all the time and continuous improvement is normal operating procedure. An idea didn't fail; it needs to be adjusted. It requires a different mind-set that's more nimble and flexible, but it can be very successful. Consider the Wright brothers and their first attempts at flight that were not successful. They studied what hadn't worked, made modifications, and tried again and again until it worked.

In the article on perpetual beta in *Public CIO*, the author says:

> The idea [of perpetual beta] has its roots in open source development, where "release and release often" has been the mantra. Tim O'Reilly, an open source advocate, has pushed the idea of perpetual beta, in which users of the software become co-developers and the software is developed in the open with new features added over time. O'Reilly has pointed to several major software services, such as Gmail, Google Maps and Flickr that have kept a beta moniker on their sites for years. ("Perpetual Beta" 2016, 12–13)

Empowerment is the second characteristic of entrepreneurial organizations. According to Ajit Ghosh (2013, 95): "Employee empowerment is the process of shifting authority and responsibility to employees at lower level in the organizational hierarchy. It is a transfer of power from the managers to their subordinates." Empowerment shows respect for colleagues, respect that they know their jobs and will make good decisions. Empowering colleagues also increases the likelihood that they will develop new ideas to improve the organization.

In *Fueled by Failure*, Jeremy Bloom says of empowerment:

> You empower people by *not* micromanaging, erring on the side of giving people general guidelines rather than explicit, detailed directions. Informed employees are more involved and empowered in a company. And the more freedom people have to take on tasks, manage them, find solutions, and execute them, the more they feel connected to and woven into the company's culture. (Bloom 2015)

According to Krautter, Lock, and Scanlon (2013), empowered people feel competent, trusted, in control, accomplished, and proud. These colleagues are more likely to come forward with ideas to improve the organization's situation, resources, and services. Empowerment means providing professional autonomy to members of the organization, but always in service of its mission. Ideas should be cleared with one's supervisor before proceeding.

From the supervisor's perspective, empowerment means communicating the mission, identifying the challenges, and letting people get on with their work. Delegating is not the same as empowering. Delegating implies the supervisor assigned work to the employee while empowerment means the idea originated with the employee. Micromanaging is the enemy of empowerment.

From the employee's perspective, when an idea comes to mind for solving a problem, filling a gap, or improving the organization, take it to one's supervisor and talk it over. Then, commit to working on the idea: create a plan, conduct background research. Finally, meet with the supervisor regularly to keep her informed, solicit her input on the idea, and obtain permission for the use of any resources that might be needed for the execution phase.

The third characteristic of entrepreneurial organizations is a reward system that's aligned with entrepreneurial behavior. As Krautter et al. say, "Reward the behavior you wish to encourage. To change behavior, change what you reward" (Krautter, Lock, and Scanlon 2013). Colleagues should be recognized for taking initiative, submitting ideas in service of the mission, and acting on them.

Rewards can be both intrinsic and extrinsic: the sense of accomplishment for the person or team that did the work or a public recognition of the work. The work that should be rewarded isn't necessarily a successfully implemented project. One of the hallmarks of an entrepreneurial organization is risk taking. Colleagues and teams should be rewarded for generating ideas, implementing new programs, and taking risks. Disappointing results should not be punished; to the contrary, the effort behind them should be rewarded. Once a disappointing outcome gets punished, the flow of good ideas will stop; few will be willing to take that risk.

Disappointing results are another opportunity, an opportunity to learn why they didn't produce the desired outcome. With that information, many projects can be modified or adjusted to obtain the desired outcome. Think back to the Google example where their philosophy is launch it, assess it, and fix it. If the organization waits to launch a perfect project, it may never be launched.

Leaders can use various rewards to encourage entrepreneurial behavior by recognizing it during annual performance evaluations and goal setting. They can create space for direct reports to develop their ideas, remove obstacles, and help find the necessary resources to implement them. From a bottom-up perspective, we can all encourage entrepreneurial behavior in our colleagues. Recognize and praise those who generate ideas and implement them. Praise from peers can be deeply meaningful. Krautter et al. suggest that in a team setting, it's important to celebrate the milestones and accomplishments, value everyone's contributions, and share the team's success stories with the whole organization (Krautter, Lock, and Scanlon 2013).

CELEBRATING THE ENTREPRENEURIAL SPIRIT IN
LIBRARIES AND LIBRARIANS

The report from the Kauffman Foundation provided the motivation to recognize and celebrate entrepreneurial activities of librarians by the authors' home institutions—Wake Forest University Libraries and the University of North Carolina at Greensboro University Libraries. A planning committee has been in place since 2008 that organizes and markets a small conference, the Conference for Entrepreneurial Librarians, dedicated to sharing and celebrating librarians' entrepreneurial spirit. The conferences have been themed and titled as follows (Conference for Entrepreneurial Librarians, n.d.):

- "Inspiration, Innovation, Celebration: A Conference for Entrepreneurial Librarians"—2009
- "From Vision to Implementation"—2011
- "Social Entrepreneurship in Action"—2013
- "Take Risks, Embrace Change!"—2014
- "Imagine the Next!"—2016

Each conference's goal was twofold: to inspire entrepreneurial action among librarians and to create a community among those who do. The institutions have shared the hosting responsibilities by alternating the conference location between the two institutions, located about thirty miles apart. Presenters and attendees have come mostly from the United States, and there has been international appeal with attendance by a handful of individuals that have come from China, Nigeria, South Africa, and England.

Each conference has featured keynote speakers who have demonstrated the leadership and vision within their own expertise and are willing to share with a new audience of interested innovators in their own right. Keynoters have been a combination of well-known librarians, who have exhibited innovation within our profession, such as Steven Bell, and local educators or business professionals, such as Dr. Dianne Welsh, who is the Hayes Distinguished Professor of Entrepreneurship and founding director of the Entrepreneurship Program at the University of North Carolina, Greensboro. This combination of talent and skill helps to address a broader point of the entrepreneurial spirit. The audience is made up largely of academic librarians, with some representation from public, special, and community college libraries. Various professional contributions have arisen from this conference, such as the aforementioned book, *The Entrepreneurial Librarian*, several articles, conference proceedings (http://libjournal.uncg.edu/index.php/pcel), and webinars and conference presentations.

Each conference ends with a recap in which one or two representatives of the host organizations convene a final session on "what we've learned." This is an intentional review of the conference activities in which planning committee members hold a discussion with the attendees about what they learned from keynoters, presenters, posters, and each other.

Conferences are assessed via a Qualtrics survey shortly after its conclusion. Participants are asked about their level of satisfaction with keynote speakers, concurrent session content, value of the material presented, sufficiency of networking opportunities, and satisfaction with the venue. Participants are also asked if they would return to a future conference and whether they would recommend it to a colleague. The conference committee holds a review meeting a month after the conference to review the survey, as well as attendance, the budget, and our sense of how we can do it better next time. All these results are captured in the minutes and become the starting point for planning the next conference.

Assessment activities conducted, related to presenters' efforts from the conferences, have demonstrated positive emotions and reinforcement of their actions through recognition that the risks individuals took in their home institutions were well received and productive enough for sharing with the larger group. Candid discussions among presenters related to barriers, roadblocks, or overall lack of organizational support have encouraged conference contributors to intensify their efforts with the next idea and not be discouraged. Likewise, a sense of excitement provided participants with the motivation to return to their home institutions with a stronger purpose for considering ideas and actions that didn't fit the current status quo.

Participants who have been repeat attendees to the conferences, or authored a proceeding or publication related to these activities, also expressed anecdotally the courage to lead and encourage others at their home institutions and to explore creative endeavors beyond their perceived boundaries. Many of these librarians have advanced in their careers or moved on to larger venues sharing their ideas and expertise.

The conference activities have also produced other forms of scholarly output including webinars, a monograph, and published articles. A complete listing that includes all activities prior to the 2016 conference is available in the appendix.

CONCLUSION

Librarians can be entrepreneurial. Librarians can be creative. Librarians can be innovative. It's a matter of having the spirit, motivation, and inspiration to look further, beyond established norms in order to stretch goals and set standards higher than the current environment might be operating at. A stagnant environment is a barrier to overcome because environments and communities should not stand still but be diverse and dynamic. Librarianship as a profession serves constituents and stakeholders seeking help and information for stakeholder creations and knowledge creation. Librarians have those same opportunities to change the profession, by creating innovative ways to provide information resources and services to our clients.

Entrepreneurial librarians are leaders who are not afraid of change and whose emotional intelligence allows for growth. They influence others and help drive organizational change as well as moving the profession forward. Organizations that foster and encourage innovative activities and support leaders to be creative will reap the benefits from professionals who make improvements to the profession. Ideas and innovative experiences should be shared by all and not be considered negative in this more dynamic society. It's the entrepreneurial spirit that drives change and improves our profession.

If the reader is interested in learning more about entrepreneurship in libraries and meeting like-minded colleagues, take advantage of these conferences and join us—they are spaced a year to a year and a half apart. You are always welcome. The website for the Conference for Entrepreneurial Librarians can be found at entrelib.org where you can find the programs and presentations from past conferences.

APPENDIX: PUBLICATIONS AND ADDITIONAL ACTIVITIES

Webinars

- 2010 Webinar: "The Roadmap to the Marketplace"
- 2012 Webinar: "Social Entrepreneurship: Digitizing our Cultural History"

September 2009 issue of *Against the Grain*

- Steven J. Bell, "The Librarian Entrepreneur: Demystifying an Oxymoron"
- Doug Boyd, "Hoops and Horses: Innovative Approaches to Oral History in a Digital Environment"
- Adam Corson-Finnerty, "Money, Money, Money"
- Anita Norton, "Library Integration through Collaboration: Partnering in the Course Development Process"
- Michael Crumpton, "Going Green in the Library: It's Not Just for Contractors"
- Jennifer Calvo, "The Learning Commons after Dark Series"

Article

Scanlon, Mary G., and Michael A. Crumpton. 2011. "Re-conceiving Entrepreneurship for Libraries: Collaboration and the Anatomy of a Conference." (Conference news.) *Collaborative Librarianship* 3 (1).

Monograph

Krautter, Mary, Mary Beth Lock, and Mary G. Scanlon. 2012. *The Entrepreneurial Librarian: Essays on the Infusion of Private-Business Dynamism into Professional Service.* Jefferson, N.C.: McFarland.

Proceedings

Take Risks, Embrace Change: The 2014 Conference for Entrepreneurial Librarians was held October 17, 2014. Links to contributed proceedings: http://libjournal.uncg.edu/index.php/pcel.

REFERENCES

Bazirjian, Rosann V. 2009. "Entrepreneurship in Libraries." *Against the Grain* 21 (4): 16–17.

Bell, Stephen J. 2009. "The Librarian Entrepreneur? Demystifying an Oxymoron." *Against the Grain* 21 (4): 18–19.

Bloom, Eric P. 2016. "Creating a Productivity Culture." *NC HR Review* (Spring/Summer): 12–13.

Bloom, Jeremy. 2015. *Fueled by Failure.* Irvine, Calif.: Entrepreneur.

Bowie, Norman. 2013. "Organizational Integrity and Moral Climates." *Business Ethics in the 21st Century* 39: 183–205.

Conference for Entrepreneurial Librarians. n.d. Retrieved from www.entrelib.org.

Cornwall, Jeffrey R., and Baron Perlman. 1990. *Organizational Entrepreneurship.* Homewood, Ill.: Richard D. Irwin.

Crumpton, Michael A. 2015. *Strategic Human Resource Planning for Academic Libraries.* Waltham, Mass.: Chandos.

Drake, Miriam A. 2000. "Technological Innovation and Organizational Change Revisited." *Journal of Academic Librarianship* 26 (1): 53–59.

Ehrlichman, Matt. 2016. "5 Characteristics of Entrepreneurial Spirit." http://www.inc.com/matt-ehrlichman/5-characteristics-of-entrepreneurial-spirit.html.

Ghosh, Ajit J. 2013. "Employee Empowerment: A Strategic Tool to Obtain Sustainable Competitive Advantage." *International Journal of Management* 30 (3): 95.

Goleman, Daniel, Richard Boyatzis, and Annie McKee. 2013. *Primal Leadership.* Cambridge, Mass.: Harvard Business Review Press.

Hernon, Peter, and Joseph R. Matthews. 2013. *Reflecting on the Future.* Chicago: American Library Association.

James, Lawrence R., Carol C. Choi, Emily Ko, Patricia K. McNeil, Matthew Minton, Maryann Wright., et al. 2007. "Organizational and Psychological Climate: A Review of Theory and Research." *European Journal of Work and Organizational Psychology* 17 (1): 5–32.

Jones, Stephanie. 2014. "How to Build an 'Intrapreneurial' Culture: An Entrepreneurial Culture within an Organization." *Effective Executive* 17 (2): 40.

Krautter, Mary, Mary Beth Lock, and Mary G. Scanlon. 2013. *The Entrepreneurial Librarian.* Jefferson, N.C.: McFarland.

———. 2015. "Developing an Entrepreneurial Organization." Presentation at the North Carolina Library Association Biennial Conference.

Mathews, Brian. 2014. "Flip the Model: Strategies for Creating and Delivering Value." *Journal of Academic Librarianship* 40: 16–24.

Mendez, Laura, and M. Esther Del Moral. 2015. "Research and Education Innovation with Video Games." *Electronic Journal of Research in Educational Psychology* 13 (2): 211–18.

"Nurturing the Entrepreneurial Spirit." National Content Standards. http://www.entre-ed.com/Standards_Toolkit/nurturing.htm.

"Perpetual Beta." 2016. *Public CIO* (Summer): 12–13.

Pierce, Sarah. 2008. "Spirit of the Entrepreneur." https://www.entrepreneur.com/article/ 190986.

Sarros, James C., Brian K. Cooper, and Joseph C. Santora. 2008. "Building a Climate for Innovation through Transformational Leadership and Organizational Culture." *Journal of Leadership & Organizational Studies* 15 (2): 145–58.

Saunders, Laura. 2015. "Academic Libraries' Strategic Plans: Top Trends and Under-recognized Areas." *Journal of Academic Librarianship* 41: 285–91.

Scanlon, Mary G., and Michael A. Crumpton. 2011. "Re-conceiving Entrepreneurship for Libraries: Collaboration and the Anatomy of a Conference." *Collaborative Librarianship* 3 (1): 16–27.

"Social Entrepreneurship: Digitizing Our Cultural History." 2012. Webinar.

Walter, Scott, and R. David Lankes. 2015. "The Innovation Agenda." *College & Research Libraries*, November, 854–58.

Wapner, Charlie. 2016. *The People's Incubator: Libraries Propel Entrepreneurship.* American Library Association. http://www.ala.org/advocacy/sited/ala.org/advocacy/files/content/ ALA_Entrepreneurship_White_ Paper_Final.pdf.

Chapter Five

The End of the World as We've Known It

Disruptive Innovation in an Academic Library

Rebecca Bichel and C. Heather Scalf

There is nothing more difficult to take in hand, more perilous to conduct, or more uncertain in its success, than to take the lead in the introduction of a new order of things.—Niccolò Machiavelli

What would academic libraries look like if they enacted the calls to action from forty years of library and business innovators? What if library leaders rejected counsel for "thoughtful change" in favor of disruptive innovation? The University of Texas at Arlington (UTA) Libraries presents one view of a library organization committed to disruptive change. While not a completed redesign, the organization offers a case study in the truth that bold action toward transformation need not trigger an organizational or institutional crisis. This chapter explores the UTA Libraries' disruptive innovation model of strategic action anchored by nimble data analysis, entrepreneurship and innovation theory, and corporate and academic best practices.

DISRUPTION THEORY

Harvard professor Clayton M. Christensen, a well-published and well-recognized expert on disruptive innovation, writes about disruption and its impact on organizational success and survival. In his groundbreaking 1997 book *The Innovator's Dilemma: When New Technologies Cause Great Firms to Fail*, Christensen presents a framework to explain why established, successful companies were unable to compete with newer and more nimble companies.

He notes two ways in which former competitive advantages became burdens for these companies: (1) new products and services were developed only in response to market data, and (2) organizational workflows and hierarchies were highly structured to maintain efficiency and consistency. Christensen labeled this mature business model as sustaining (Christensen 1997). When nimble start-ups, able to innovate quickly and willing to be disruptive rather than responsive, entered an industry composed of sustaining companies, the sustaining companies lost. Academic libraries should heed these lessons and not wait to act until users ask for a service. Libraries need to be proactive entrepreneurs, dismantling policies and bureaucracies that stifle invention, creative thinking, and innovative action.

If the backbone of sustaining technologies is market analysis and customer feedback, the heart of disruptive technologies is the idea that it is not customer satisfaction or feedback that drives service changes assessed and analyzed, but rather a deep understanding of the work that the customer is trying to accomplish. Recognizing this, UTA Libraries engaged in a critical environmental scan in 2012 using a variety of approaches, including focus groups, spatial observational data, transactional analysis, and more. The goal was to deepen library staff understanding of faculty and student behaviors, priorities, and needs, rather than ask about their satisfaction with library collections, spaces, or services. Disruptive systems are not targeted at what customers say they want but on solving customers' problems.

HISTORY

In 1973, the Conference Board, a well-known global, independent business research association, asked management experts to predict the major management challenges for the next twenty years. One finding stands out for its relevance almost a half century later for academic libraries: "An acceleration in the rate of change will result in an increasing need for reorganization. Reorganization is usually feared, because it means disturbance of the status quo, a threat to people's vested interests in their jobs, and an upset to established ways of doing things. For these reasons, needed reorganization is often deferred, with a resulting loss in effectiveness and an increase in costs" (Bower and Walton 1973, 126).

In 2012 the UTA Libraries faced the same opportunities and challenges as many of its peers. In the opportunity category: increasing enrollment, high gate counts, campus respect for traditional library roles, and a new campus culture valuing innovation and risk taking. In the challenges category: steep inflation for serial publications, a flat budget, declining reference statistics, low use of the legacy print collection, a library culture comfortable with the status quo, and little role or voice in university strategic planning. While

UTA Libraries faced the same environment as other academic libraries, the organization's leadership chose to embrace the campus culture of experimentation and selected disruptive innovation as the path forward. This stands in real contrast to the choice by many academic libraries to defer change or pursue a slow path of change, hoping to minimize disruption to staff and/or users.

Carla Stoffle, Robert Renaud, and Jerilyn R. Veldof effectively describe contrasting perspectives on change in their 1996 article "Choosing Our Futures." The authors note that one view holds that little or no organizational change is needed in libraries because current structures are adequate. "The countervailing view of the future that the authors hold is that academic libraries must change—fundamentally and irreversibly—what they do and how they do it, and that these changes need to come quickly. Change is going to occur continuously and the pace of change is likely to increase rather than decrease indefinitely into the future. To be successful under these conditions, libraries must reshape the prevailing corporate culture" (Stoffle, Renaud, and Veldof 1996, 213).

Stoffle et al. identify elements of the culture that academic libraries need to abandon: (1) a focus on acquiring, processing, and storing physical objects, (2) an aversion to risk taking that assumes it is better to miss an opportunity than make a mistake, and (3) a tendency to work in isolation on library, rather than institutional, goals. This twenty-year-old description still fits too many academic libraries today. *College & Research Libraries* recognized the current relevance of this essay by including it in their seventy-fifth-anniversary issue in 2015 (Stoffle, Renaud, and Veldof 2015, 316–27).

Some readers might respond that there is little resistance to change in libraries today, while also cautioning that libraries need to be *thoughtful* in their approach to change. In this instance, *thoughtful* is a euphemism for *slow*. It is precisely this aversion to risk that Stoffle et al. identified. To echo the experts at the College Board, delays have a cost. Deliberate disruption *is* a method for thoughtful change. This chapter examines how deliberate disruption unfolded at UTA using the three cultural barriers that Stoffle and her colleagues identified.

The first culture change that the "Choosing Our Futures" authors identified was a move from an acquisition culture. An immediate challenge when moving from acquisition to access is that librarians often have their professional identities wrapped up in collection-building activities. Some see this activity as a unique intellectual contribution of the librarian to the academy. Meanwhile, the Association of Research Libraries (ARL) rankings continue to reinforce the cultural importance of acquisition.

In 2010, UTA Libraries leaders were asked to detail the projected cost for UTA to pursue ARL status, recognizing that this could be one recognized benchmark of excellence. Based upon that analysis, both university and library leadership agreed that the massive acquisition investment required did not advance the university's strategic goals.

Unhampered by the behavioral expectations driven by ARL rankings, in 2014 UTA Libraries analyzed the costs and outputs of the organization's existing just-in-case acquisition model. An analysis of the UTA Libraries' print book purchasing and usage patterns from 2000 to 2013 found that 42 percent of new books had never circulated, and that 84 percent of the entire circulating book collection had not been checked out by anyone for the past ten years. Pairing this with data on declining circulation rates created a compelling call to action. While many libraries were piloting on-demand programs, no large academic library had wholly adopted on demand as the monographic purchase model. After consulting with the university president, provost, and academic deans, UTA Libraries did just that. The just-in-time model initiated in 2014 allows the libraries to grant access to a wide collection of e-books and print book records through a discovery layer. Once selected by a user, an item is purchased. The acquisition policy prefers electronic books, but where print is the best or only option, print records display and, when selected, books ship with minimal delay using Amazon Prime. Demand-driven acquisition (DDA) has made it possible to target book purchases to items directly selected by UTA faculty and students, so each dollar spent has impact. Focusing on the strategic plan, the libraries are engaging faculty with a new suite of scholarly communication services while continuing to provide highly responsive on-demand and ILL (interlibrary loan) services. To paraphrase Kurt Andersen, author of the 2009 book *Reset*, "This *is* the end of the world as we've known it [in libraries]. But it isn't the end of the world" (Andersen 2009, 17).

Stoffle, Renaud, and Veldof (1996, 213–25) call for libraries to embrace risk taking and to truly engage with university priorities. James Neal reminds us of this in his 2015 preface to the reprint of the Stoffle et al. article when he notes that there still "is too much strategic planning and not enough strategic thinking and action. . . . Our academic library program planning is too often not linked to institutional planning" (Neal 2015, 314).

At UTA, the libraries' and university's strategic plans are companion documents, and they read as a tightly integrated duo. Library leaders contributed to the creation of the university's plan, serving on multiple university strategic planning task forces. The full fifty-five-page plan for the university is available online at https://www.uta.edu/strategicplan/ and includes the following vision: "The University of Texas at Arlington is an internationally recognized research university, distinguished by excellence and access through transformative knowledge production and education based on scholarship, collaboration, innovation, creativity, and global impact" (University of Texas at Arlington 2015). The libraries' plan was written with a set of imperatives designed to catalyze university goals. The libraries' vision, which served as a model for UTA's president in their planning process, supports the larger organization's approach: "The UTA Libraries are committed to equipping scholars to successfully connect, create, explore, and innovate in the new information ecosystem through extraordinary access, creative collaborations, impactful services, transformational technologies and inspiring spaces" (University of Texas at Arlington Libraries 2016).

While developing data-driven outcomes throughout the plan, the leadership team acknowledged the discomfort caused by taking action with abbreviated data gathering. The reality at UTA is that decision making must be highly accountable and nimble. In the face of ambitious goals, UTA leaders see the delay of decision making for the pursuit of more and more-perfect data as a white whale, the enemy of strategic action. The expected mode of operation is that data is collected for a short, reasonable time, and then *data drives action*. This expectation recognizes that the pursuit of perfect data is actually a pursuit of certainty. In rapidly changing environments, there is no certainty. Honoring this, UTA Libraries publicly celebrate risk taking paired with time-limited data gathering as the organizational expectation. With the pairing of data-driven action and risk taking, UTA Libraries' strategic plan is the launchpad for deep organizational disruption.

Christensen speaks not just to the creation process. He also describes a process of creative destruction supported by disruptive innovation that allows for the rise of newer, more efficient and effective processes as more sluggish functions and processes wither. The reallocation of resources that follows allows for creative construction of more relevant and agile products and opportunities. UTA Libraries' experience is that few activities are as challenging as trying to dismantle a long-standing service or process. Without an organizational process for "creative destruction" at UTA Libraries, such decisions were avoided or held at the unit rather than organization level. For example, a data-driven decision around 2010 by the serials unit to stop serial check-in to allow resources to be directed to other, more impactful services did not end the process. Well-intentioned reference staff decided the service was still needed and adopted the workflow. There was no organizational conversation and decision making, so no freeing of overall resources.

In their 2004 article, Susan Lafferty and Jenny Edwards look at the applicability of Christensen's research to higher education and libraries (Lafferty and Edwards 2004, 252–58). The advent of the Internet has fostered great disruption in the academic environment, and specifically in libraries. While libraries have long been viewed as the authoritative source for reliable information, the ubiquity of Google as a search engine and information provider has forced libraries into a battle for relevance. Embracing Christensen's sustaining model, libraries continue on a path to incrementally increase their value to the customer. Rather than only providing books and other materials, libraries worked to move upmarket with newer collections, relevant programs and services, catchy marketing, and events. Once it became clear that the Internet was here to stay, libraries adopted and adapted digital technology to continue to provide value to customers. In spite of these efforts, Lafferty and Edwards posit that even if universities manage to survive, it may well be that their libraries disappear, unless they engage in dramatic, and disruptive, change. They too urge action, calling for libraries to "become part of the disruption and thrive into the future" (Lafferty and Edwards 2004, 258). They then close wondering aloud if libraries will act.

STRATEGIC INNOVATIONS AT UTA

With an expanding universe of technological change clearly visible, the UTA libraries chose the role of disruptor, looking to create new products that would be valued by the community and enhance their academic and professional success in a way that no other entity on campus has yet done. Bringing this form of innovation to the campus has been controversial among some library staff. Creative construction initiatives to build innovations that will provide value to the community are complicated by a reluctance to engage in creative destruction to shed processes and functions that do not contribute to the vision.

In support of the university's priority of student success, the libraries initiated partnerships with academic support stakeholders, such as academic advisors and tutors, to create the Academic Plaza in the Central Library. The Academic Plaza offers textbooks on reserve for courses with the highest number of drops, failures, or withdrawals; tutoring; supplemental instruction; writing consultations and workshops; and academic advising. It hosts faculty office hours and a dedicated space for student veterans to collaborate. Recognized as a Hispanic-serving institution (HSI), the university was awarded a highly competitive, five-year $2.62 million Department of Education grant to enhance services for nontraditional students. The grant funded the creation of a new center in the libraries' Academic Plaza as a resource to increase graduation and retention rates among Hispanic and lower-income students. Transfer students find resources available at the Transfer UTA Center in the Academic Plaza.

The libraries' strategic plan targets a range of new services for advanced scholars. New positions were created to support emerging forms of scholarly communication, focusing on digital humanities, open education resources, publishing, and data research. The libraries have provided leadership in offering workshops, online educational materials, and consultations for faculty to support compliance with public access mandates, such as those from the National Institutes of Health (U.S. Department of Health and Human Services 2016).

Through specific strategic goals to support the professional success of faculty, the libraries have engaged broadly across campus with activities as varied as presenting to faculty writing circles, creating videos to support librarian integration into classes, and participating in campus-wide professional learning communities. A delivery service to bring requested titles to faculty offices was expanded in 2015 to include PhD students. Beginning in 2016–2017, the libraries will provide article publishing and subvention funds for UTA scholars, shifting investment from downstream acquisition to support upstream creation of scholarship.

One of the most ambitious undertakings has been the creation of the UTA FabLab. Beyond making available a broad array of STEAM (science, technology, engineering, arts, and mathematics) technology to inspire creativity, the libraries created a partner department for experiential learning. These librarians collaborate with faculty to integrate maker literacies and experiential learning opportunities into university coursework and create informal, autodidactic opportunities for users to "learn through play." For example, a series of pop-up workshops branded as the "LifeHack College Series" offer UTA students low-risk opportunities to use FabLab technologies in fun ways to solve everyday challenges. These efforts are growing in success, as faculty from a variety of disciplines across campus integrate the FabLab into their courses and students pursue independent, entrepreneurial endeavors. Users are able to manifest their own original ideas and designs, which they can then use as evidence of marketability and skills when entering the job market. A full-time staff position was created for an embedded artist-maker to lead public art projects and engage users across skill sets and disciplines in collaborative creation, changing a STEM focus in the FabLab to a STEAM focus. The libraries' maker literacies librarian, along with FabLab staff and campus faculty, has created a task force to further validate and promote how the hard and soft skills gleaned in the FabLab promote student success.

Looking across all of these disruptive innovations, none were initiated by a specific user request. Library staff studied the campus environment and emerging practices globally, and proactively acted. And all of these new initiatives were launched within a three-year window filled with many other firsts for the organization.

LIBRARY AS ENTREPRENEUR

Brian Mathews's *Facing the Future: Think Like a Startup* (Mathews 2012) has been both inspirational and controversial in the profession. Following thought leaders before him, his is an urgent call to action for libraries. Mathews goes beyond calling for bold change to even contextualize the limitation of the typical safe, incremental changes librarians make as "vacuum-cleaner-thinking" (Mathews 2012). Rather than focusing on improvements to what already is, think of what the user is trying to do. Is the goal of using the vacuum cleaner to use the tool more efficiently, or to have clean floors? His co-opting of the anthropological term "liminality" (meaning "the ambiguous state of being between states of being" [Barfield 2000, 288]) to describe the new normal for organizations who engage in disruption is at once elegant and spot on. Leadership coaches Marsha Clark and Jerry Magar prepared the UTA Libraries leadership team for the emotional swings by staff as they moved through the stages of grief with a model called "the change curve" (see figure 5.1). This was derived from a grief model developed by Elisabeth Kübler-Ross (1969). During the transition time when so many colleagues were grieving past roles, the leadership team adopted an inelegant but far more descriptive sobriquet: the hell curve.

Mathews cautions against the trend to hire a few change agents and expect change to bloom. "We can't expect entrepreneurialism to flourish in a tradition-obsessed environment. We can't just talk about change; it must be embedded in the actions of employees. Innovation is a team sport" (Mathews 2012, 3). Echoing Christensen, Mathews exhorts libraries to move to a start-

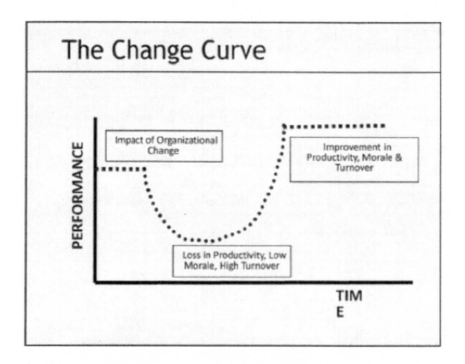

Figure 5.1.   A representation of the change curve applied to organizational performance. *Source: Marsha Clark & Associates, 2012*

up culture, a culture around "what's next" rather than "what's now." He notes that in such a culture, realizing when you need to make a change is critical, and he cautions that plans need to be living documents, which change to serve larger goals. UTA Libraries engaged in such an updating of the strategic plan, maintaining the core vision but documenting rerouting and new opportunities. The first draft of the plan in 2014 was a model of Mathews's advice to "plant many seeds" (Mathews 2012, 5) and nurture those that show potential. The document "seized the white space" (Mathews 2012, 5) suggesting opportunities far beyond libraries' traditional roles. This experience showed that what was intended as a garden of possibilities may be ill received by others as an overly long "to-do" list.

Another entrepreneurial tool the UTA Libraries use to facilitate innovation is referred to as a "pivot." Today's most successful start-ups are comfortable launching new products and services before they gain a dataset comprehensive enough to support ideal decision making. These organizations instead use the momentum of action to allow them to gather more complete and/or meaningful data, which may be altered by the changing external environment during rollouts anyway, and pivoting toward new directions if and when necessary. The term "pivot" is useful to clarify that course corrections do not signal a change in vision or lack of vision. Pivots are adjustments to a strategy that are responsive to current data and at the same time are grounded in an ongoing vision. It is common for leaders at UTA Libraries to be asked to respond to some version of this comment: "You are making more changes. Make up your mind." To some, any change from an initial strategy announcement is seen as retrenchment or change run amok. The correct answer for UTA Libraries is: "Yes, more changes are coming. This is what it looks like to move forward strategically while learning. This is the *new normal* for our organization." We might say more succinctly, "Welcome to liminality. It's the new normal."

UTA Libraries have had several pivots since reorganizing and adopting a new vision in 2013. Beyond cautioning library leaders against chasing customer satisfaction, Christensen also warns of the limitations of outdated organizational charts. To enable strategic prioritization, UTA Libraries made a dramatic redesign to the organizational chart in 2013, reflecting a focus on creativity, collaboration, innovation, and exploration (see appendix). Subsequent revisions to the organization chart reflect strategic pivots. One example has been in response to attempts to find the right strategy to accelerate the recognition and use of the extraordinary scholarship and creative works of UTA scholars, the libraries' first strategic imperative. An initial strategy intended to align liaison roles to facilitate this goal fell short. Still committed to the goal, the leadership team pivoted to another strategy. This advanced the initiative somewhat but did not yet meet either the libraries' or faculty members' heightened expectations. January 2016 saw a third pivot. Same end goal but a different path based on more data. Now the organization is investing heavily in collaborating with faculty to develop and promote their digital identities. A new scholarly communication team is in place to partner with the liaisons and deepen their expertise on emerging forms of scholarship, such as digital humanities. The hope is that this third pivot found the successful strategy. Analysis of impact will guide the next steps. To provide a second example, the libraries created a new department in January 2016 to provide leadership for experiential learning in the libraries. Why was it a pivot? Leaders saw a gap in progress toward the vision for embedding maker and creative skills in the curriculum. Rather than revert to the past model of an Information Literacy Department that did not match current university goals, a new Experiential Learning Department will focus instruction initiatives around problem-based learning and actively work with faculty and members of the FabLab team to develop maker literacies and assignments grounded in these literacies.

The desire to foster a culture of innovation drove UTA library leadership to encourage two new behaviors that have not historically been part of the organization's broad culture. First, staff are expected to engage in smart risk taking, as a path to innovation. This is a conscious choice to focus on the attempt, not just the result, by celebrating staff efforts to innovate whether they lead to success or failure. In doing so, staff have a safe space to grow more comfortable with risk. Second, the organization embraces perpetual beta, or what Eric Ries describes as a "build-measure-learn" feedback loop (Ries n.d.). The concept is to avoid lengthy development timelines for new programs and services, recognizing that the pursuit of perfect data and a perfect service is costly. As Ries notes on the Lean Startup website (http://theleanstartup.com/principles): "Too many startups begin with an idea for a product that they think people want. They then spend months, sometimes years, perfecting that product without ever showing the product, even in a very rudimentary form, to the prospective customer" (Ries n.d.). Replace the word "startups" with libraries and you describe a common scenario. For example, how many library task forces have spent months or years perfecting library catalogs before releasing them for users to try? These recent pivots at UTA Libraries are an acknowledgment that the organization is operating by entrepreneurial rules, taking risks in leadership, and learning from mistakes. The constant is to learn and always move forward grounded in the strategic vision. If that forward motion requires a new strategy, then the organization pivots.

CONCLUSION

When interviewing potential library colleagues, the libraries' dean talks openly and intentionally about a culture of strategic disruption and radical transformation. Successes and failures are shared. Candidates are cautioned that while "innovation" and "risk taking" are buzzwords today, they should only consider joining UTA Libraries if they can embrace the reality of this culture: radical redesign is messy. Candidates are told that the organization has chosen to value risk taking as the path to innovation, and colleagues are expected to engage in decision making without perfect data.

UTA Libraries are still in motion—moving toward a broader adoption of disruptive practices. At the same time, no single disruptive technique has been perfected. Grounded by and passionate for the organizational vision, colleagues are applying corporate and academic theory, best national practices, and local data as the formula for disruptive innovation. Like the university mascot, UTA Libraries staff are expected to be mavericks, using a rich mix of data and dreaming to drive action. The new normal is strategic disruption.

APPENDIX: UT ARLINGTON LIBRARIES ORGANIZATION CHARTS, 2011–2016

Figure 5.2.   UTA Libraries Organization Chart 2011.

Rebecca Bichel and C. Heather Scalf

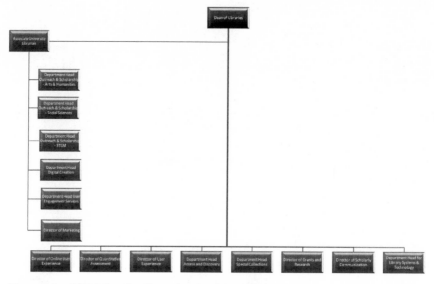

Figure 5.3.   UTA Libraries Organization Chart 2013.

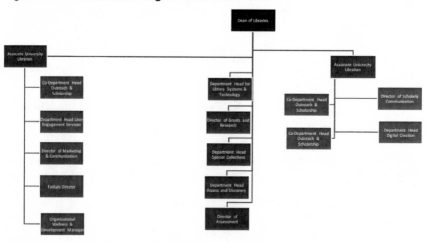

Figure 5.4.   UTA Libraries Organization Chart 2015.

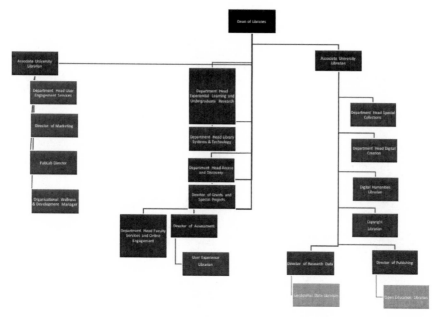

Figure 5.5. UTA Libraries Organization Chart 2016.

REFERENCES

Andersen, Kurt. 2009. *Reset: How This Crisis Can Restore Our Values and Renew America.* New York: Random House.

Barfield, Thomas J. 2000. *The Dictionary of Anthropology.* Cambridge, Mass.: Wiley.

Bower, Marvin, and C. Lee Walton. 1973. "Gearing a Business to the Future." In *Challenge to Leadership: Managing in a Changing World*, edited by Edward Collins and Conference Board. New York: Free Press.

Christensen, Clayton M. 1997. *The Innovator's Dilemma: When New Technologies Cause Great Firms to Fail.* Boston: Harvard Business School Press.

Kübler-Ross, Elisabeth 1969. *On Death and Dying.* New York: Macmillan.

Lafferty, Susan, and Jenny Edwards. 2004. "Disruptive Technologies: What Future Universities and Their Libraries?" *Library Management* 25 (6/7): 252–58.

Mathews, Brian. 2012. *Facing the Future: Think Like a Startup.* Blacksburg: Va.: VTech-Works. https://vtechworks.lib.vt.edu/bitstream/handle/10919/18649/Think%20like%20a%20STARTUP.pdf?sequence=1&isAllowed=y.

Neal, James. 2015. "Still 'Choosing Our Futures': How Many Apples in the Seed?" *College & Research Libraries* 76 (3): 310–15.

Ries, Eric. "The Lean Startup Methodology." n.d. Accessed 2016. http://theleanstartup.com/principles.

Stoffle, Carla, Robert Renaud, and Jerilyn Veldof. 1996. "Choosing Our Futures." *College & Research Libraries* 57 (3): 213–25.

———. 2015. "Choosing Our Futures." *College & Research Libraries* 76 (3): 316–27. doi:10.5860/crl.76.3.316.

University of Texas at Arlington. 2015. *Bold Solutions, Global Impact: The Modern 21st-Century University Strategic Plan.* Arlington, Tex. https://www.uta.edu/strategicplan/.

University of Texas at Arlington Libraries. 2016. *Plunging Forward: The University of Texas at Arlington 2020 Strategic Plan*. Arlington, Tex. https://library.uta.edu/sites/default/files/assessment/UT%20Arlington%20Libraries%202014-2020%20Strategic%20Plan.pdf.

U.S. Department of Health and Human Services. 2016. "NIH Public Access Policy Details." NIH Public Access Policy. Last modified March 25, 2016. http://publicaccess.nih.gov/policy.htm.

Chapter Six

Creating Spaces for Innovation in the Workplace

Michael Rodriguez

When libraries create innovative spaces—or spaces for innovation—they are mostly public-facing spaces. They might be learning commons, makerspaces, collaboration rooms, digital production labs, 3D printing stations, innovation studios, kiosks, incubators, and other buzzwords for physical spaces designed to foster creative productivity through technology and collaboration. User experience is among the hottest of job titles, and the user-first mentality is helping libraries to survive and thrive. At the same time, these transformations have the effect of framing library innovation as heavily public facing and presenting innovation in terms of technology adoption and makerspaces. Spaces that foster intraorganizational, entrepreneurial innovation by library workers are no less essential yet are largely overlooked in the literature and in practice.

How and why should libraries create spaces to foster innovation within the organization? To answer, this chapter draws on studies, concepts, and models from inside and outside the library world, buttressing that research with the author's own experiences in academic libraries. This chapter makes the case for spaces as vital to creating and sustaining innovation cultures in library organizations. How can libraries build serendipity and agility into workplace design? How can they draw on technologies to brainstorm, collaborate, and track ideas and projects? How can they sweep away physical and mental clutter to free up brainpower and time—and money—for innovation? This chapter seeks to demonstrate to library leaders at all levels how to design safe, engaging, and adaptable workplace environments that foster entrepreneurship while underscoring the positive outcomes for the organization, for staff, and for end users.

INNOVATION AND INTRAPRENEURSHIP

Definitions are a prerequisite for understanding the value and impact of innovation spaces in the workplace. "Innovation" means to convert concepts into new processes or products, or to make existing processes or products more effective or efficient, with transformational potential for the organization doing the innovating (Castree, Kitchin, and Rogers 2013). Innovation is a "core renewal process" that enables organizations to evolve their products and services continuously to lead or align with consumer markets or, in the case of libraries, user needs (Baregheh, Rowley, and Sambrook 2006, 1324). The term "spaces" simply means physical or online environments, be they offices, buildings, studios, or software applications.

Next, librarians must differentiate "innovative spaces" from "innovation spaces." Like the Guggenheim Museum's spiral interior, innovative spaces may be novel or exciting but do not necessarily foster innovative work being done in those spaces. The key question, then, is not whether a space features innovative or creative design but rather whether the design fosters innovation or creative output, and how it does so. Recognizing this distinction, Louise Bloom and Romily Faulkner (2016, 1371–87) define "innovation spaces" as "physical or virtual spaces that enable and support creative problem solving (technological or otherwise) of those who participate in the space." This definition highlights the collaborative, communal aspect of innovation spaces and notes the frequent technological component without making technology a prerequisite for innovation—a key distinction in the era of triumphalist makerspaces and digital production labs. This definition is also open ended, applying to spaces designed for use by patrons or librarians alike.

This is another key point—innovation spaces should foster creative problem solving *by the librarians*. This need is commonly overlooked. Most staff sit in static offices and cubicles or at service desks. Staff spaces have not been transformed alongside public-use spaces, and clear-cut incentives are lacking for administrators to prioritize the transformation of employee spaces. Real disincentives exist for administrators of publicly owned libraries in towns and universities, which frequently face pressure to curtail the salaries and benefits of public employees. Spending taxpayer money to craft what critics may see as lavish and unnecessary workspaces may be seen as too politically fraught a road for administrators to tread. This chapter contends otherwise.

Innovation spaces power intrapreneurship—initiatives, spearheaded by staff rather than administrators, to revitalize organizations from within by creating new or improved products, services, or processes (de Jong and Wennekers 2008, 4). Intrapreneurship includes traits such as risk taking, creative problem solving, and proactive behavior (Felício, Rodrigues, and Caldeirinha 2012, 1717–38). As Anthony Molaro, a professor of library and information science at St. Catherine University, points out, the entrepreneurial spirit is not nearly as widespread as it should be in libraries, which tend to be slow-moving bureaucracies that follow innovations rather than source them (Molaro 2013). "A large organization," notes management authority Peter F. Drucker, "is effective through its mass rather than through its agility" (Drucker 2003, 99). The implication is that innovation works slowly when it takes place in the form of top-down, bureaucratic directives. The key is to create physical and mental spaces that encourage and support intrapreneurship and that enable innovation to develop organically within even the most cumbersome bureaucracies.

INNOVATION SPACES IN LIBRARIES

As design consultant Elliott Felix observes, "Models of innovative, effective staff work spaces are rare, perhaps because attention to such spaces is itself rare." Exceptions include the James B. Hunt Jr. Library at North Carolina State University (NCSU), which colocates and mixes staff from various departments and fosters collaboration with shared informal workspaces. The Powell Library's Inquiry Labs at the University of California at Los Angeles integrate staff and user spaces (Felix 2015). The University of Connecticut's Hartford Campus Library will share a building with the city's public library and develop shared spaces for public and academic users as well as librarians. The fourth floor at Chattanooga Public Library is a public makerspace that doubles as innovation beta space and ground zero for the library's user experience designers (Goldenson and Hill 2013). However, such models are rare, or at least not widely discussed, compared to the plethora of public-facing innovation spaces. The library literature on workplace innovation spaces is also lacking, aside from a handful of magazine articles, conference presentations, and strategic plans (Bostick and Irwin 2015). These exceptions notwithstanding, most libraries of all types simply have not invested thought and resources into creating innovation spaces for staff. This is unfortunate, as spaces have a real impact on the workers who inhabit them—and on the organizations that in turn rely on those workers.

SPACES IMPACT WORKERS

"Physical space is the biggest lever to encourage collaboration," notes human analytics authority Ben Waber (Stewart 2013). Spaces bring individuals together or keep them separated. Serendipitous encounters between coworkers who have different roles or departments foster cross-fertilization of ideas and talent. People can enjoy inhabiting a physical space, or they can take refuge from inhospitable environments by mentally clocking out long before 5:00

p.m. Open floor plans and colocated staff foster interactions but also distractions, while cubicle partitions and enclosed offices foster isolation but also concentration. Green spaces—as simple as opened blinds or strategically placed indoor plants—are strongly correlated with decreased stress and improved physical and mental health (Largo-Wight et al. 2011, 124–30). NCSU's library master plan highlights the need of library workers for "open and collaborative work environments that are driven not by hierarchy but rather by evolving functional groupings and their entrepreneurial culture" in order to better deliver exceptional user experiences and satisfy user needs in the context of a twenty-first-century university library (North Carolina State University 2008).

As NCSU notes, exceptional spaces facilitate productivity and engagement among staff. Employers with highly engaged workers, defined as "those who are involved in, enthusiastic about, and committed to their work," reported 21 percent higher productivity and 10 percent higher customer ratings than organizations with the least engaged workers. These employers also experienced significantly lower turnover, absenteeism, and quality control problems. Yet in 2013 a Gallup workplace survey discovered that 70 percent of workers across all industries in the United States either are not engaged or are actively disengaged from their work (Gallup 2013, 12). Comparably, a 2007 *Library Journal* survey found that only 70 percent of academic and public librarians expressed satisfaction with their work situations. That percentage dipped to 61 percent for workers under age thirty, amid frustrations over inadequate pay, red tape, and unresponsive management (Berry 2007, 26–29). While satisfaction is not identical to engagement, administrators should not assume that newer librarians will persist in a field about which they are both passionate and dissatisfied. NCSU recognizes this. Its master plan singles out flexible, inviting staff spaces as vital to recruiting and retaining exceptional library staff (North Carolina State University 2008, 43).

CHALLENGES

In contrast to private-sector models like Google or Facebook, libraries commonly operate on shoestring budgets and are departments of larger organizations, ranging from city and county governments to universities and school systems. Library needs often struggle to compete with athletics, public safety, and other spending priorities for these organizations. This makes it challenging for libraries to absorb the costs of incentivizing employees or investing in spaces for innovation, which critics may see as "perks" for overcompensated public employees. Then, too, innovation is simply not a priority for libraries that struggle to find the budget or personnel to accomplish even routine daily work. Additionally, skepticism toward the *Library Journal* Mover & Shaker Award is symptomatic of some librarians' preference for so-called workhorses, whose focus is routine work within existing prescribed procedures, over disruptive innovators, though routine and innovation are not mutually exclusive and should coexist in most workplaces (Manley 2011). Finally, librarianship's commendable emphasis on end-user experience and customer service may contribute to the shortchanging of staff when library administrators decide where to invest. Consequently, writes design consultant Elliot Felix, libraries "have created daylit, inspiring, and reconfigurable collaborative spaces for students while just down the hall staff work in dismal, disconnected cubicle farms that lack meeting spaces, technology, variety, and flexibility" (Felix 2015).

FLEXIBLE SPACES

Another challenge to improving staff spaces is the fact that no consensus exists on what constitutes optimal innovation spaces. Most models emphasize collaboration—but sometimes, when diving into a spreadsheet, configuring a software program, or drafting a contract, workers need to concentrate rather than collaborate. Open floor plans are all the rage in the technology industry, but many workers, including the introverts who make up an estimated 63 percent of library workers, experience open offices as overwhelming and distracting (Scherdin and Beaubien 1995, 35–38; Cain 2012, 265). Neurodiverse workers, for example, with attention deficit/hyperactivity disorder or on the autism spectrum, commonly struggle to concentrate and be creative amid ambient noise, visual stimuli, or other environmental distractions. Workers with diverse needs and tasks require equally varied workspaces (Morris, Begel, and Wiedermann 2015, 177).

To accommodate these needs and optimize employee performance, libraries should permit use of noise-canceling headphones, designate close-doored or acoustically private offices for focused work or as "quiet spaces" for workers to rest or recharge their social batteries, and offer workers a range of spaces that should include enclosed offices or cubicles away from foot traffic. Some workplaces may wish to install white noise machines (Morris, Begel, and Wiedermann 2015). Innovation is best fostered via a mix of spaces optimized for individual or collaborative work, flexible enough to accommodate either, and connected enough to facilitate collaborative and serendipitous interactions among staff (Kristal 2014).

SERENDIPITOUS SPACES

"The biggest driver of performance in complex industries like software," claims human analytics researcher Ben Waber, "is serendipitous interaction"—not premeditated get-togethers but rather fortuitous interactions leading to idea exchange and opportunities for collaboration and innovation (Stewart 2013). Insofar as libraries resemble the software industry, the argument is apt. The author once dropped by a colleague's office to say hello; the conversation morphed into an electrifying conversation, involving whiteboard and spreadsheet activity, which could ultimately transform how end users accessed the library's electronic resources. A University of Michigan study found that when researchers' walking patterns overlapped—say, walking from the office to the restroom—collaborations jumped by up to 20 percent for every hundred feet of "zonal overlap" (Swanbrow 2012). Google designs its spaces to maximize these serendipitous interactions. "We want it to be easy [for] Googlers to collaborate and bump into each other," explained a Google spokesperson. Serendipity involved everything from installing indoor volleyball courts to arranging cafeteria tables so that colleagues are more likely to physically bump into each other, triggering spontaneous interactions (Silverman 2013).

No library is going to install indoor volleyball courts for staff. However, there are many inexpensive, low-key ways to foster serendipitous interaction. Common practice is to colocate one department's staff in the same office space; this colocation promotes collaboration within that department. But more importantly, departments should not be isolated from one another on different floors with several flights of stairs between staff and serendipity. The previously cited University of Michigan study also found that collaborations increased 33 percent among researchers inhabiting the same building and 50 percent among researchers inhabiting the same floor (Swanbrow 2012). As many staff as practicable should be colocated, with restrooms, elevators, kitchens, and other common spaces positioned to maximize serendipitous interaction. Common spaces should be improved with comfortable seating, indoor plants, art, and other pleasantries to encourage workers to feel comfortable and engaged in those spaces. Open offices similarly foster serendipity, but noise and other distractions associated with open offices can undercut productivity, and lack of privacy can feel uncomfortable. A more egalitarian approach is to give workers spatial choice and flexibility.

EMPLOYEE-DRIVEN SPACES

Human-centered design generally posits workers as oppressed by inefficient structures. To the rescue of this "worker-as-victim" come the heroic information designers to create better systems and structures. But how much do workers need imposed structures in the first place? Individual workers inevitably "assert their own agency" by adapting and innovating systems and spaces on the fly (Spinuzzi 2003, 1–5). Actual users of workspaces should lead or actively consult with any designs, while organizations should design or renovate workspaces with the built-in flexibility to accommodate ad hoc changes. Library leadership should foster employee-driven spaces.

Satisfied, productive workers are typically those who exercise some degree of control and autonomy, or agency, over their work and space. Are workers permitted to customize their workspaces? Are they free to choose between a laptop and a desktop, Mac or PC, a standing desk or a sitting desk? Can they roam and work, locating themselves in the café or atrium rather than in their cubicles? Are workers empowered to work flextime or telecommute occasionally? Are there flex spaces—unclaimed offices or even a couch with nearby electrical outlets—to accommodate workers who wish to disrupt their routines to think more creatively? Are moveable whiteboards, projector carts, or poster easels provided in shared spaces to facilitate impromptu meetings, mapping, and brainstorming? Are teams free to shuffle chairs and tables into optimized seating arrangements? Are workspaces able to be made colorful or engaging to forestall ennui resulting from endless gray cubicle walls? Does library leadership care how or where employees work, as long as the work is done and done well? In short, do workers exercise agency over their spaces?

COLLABORATIVE SPACES

Like employee-driven spaces, collaborative spaces are adaptable and driven by choice and spontaneity. Spaces for focused individual work should be created along with spaces for teamwork. "Like a great city," writes Felix, "space needs to transition from lively to quiet and be organized into 'neighborhoods'" (Felix 2015). But most library spaces are configured for individual work—think of the cubicles or enclosed offices that predominate in the average library. Collaborative spaces are largely limited to staff meeting rooms. These rooms might contain a table and chairs and a large computer monitor or projector screen. Libraries should reconceptualize these rooms as collaboration spaces, adding jacks so that more than one laptop can be connected, adding more than one computer monitor or touch screen, and adding whiteboards or smartboards so staff can sketch or scrawl to visualize complex ideas and plans. Huddle rooms—small spaces for impromptu meetings and equipped with technology—are essential for teams. Some rooms may be left without furniture to facilitate so-called stand-up meetings—a technique commonly used by today's "agile" project teams, during which participants must remain standing as a physical reminder to keep discussions brief. Libraries should also equip collaborative spaces with tools for remote collaboration, such as Skype or Google Hangouts, or even hold meetings entirely in virtual spaces.

VIRTUAL SPACES

Video conferencing brings us to the next key point: virtual innovation spaces. E-mails and traditional meetings are tremendous drains on productivity, while circular conversations and long-winded e-mails are mentally draining to boot. Emerging technologies such as Slack, Trello, and Asana not only streamline communication but also facilitate brainstorming, collaboration, and exchange of ideas. Slack is a cloud-based collaboration application that cuts down on e-mails and nonessential meetings through messaging, private or team based, on "channels" or groups that users set up. Trello and Asana are team project management tools that go beyond the to-do list to facilitate collaboration and information sharing, again, without e-mail. Other essential tools might include OneDrive or Google Drive, which enable document sharing and concurrent editing and tracking of changes, alongside secure team file sharing platforms like FileLocker or Box.

DECLUTTERED SPACES

Physical and virtual spaces alike are prone to disorganization and clutter. Every worker has witnessed inboxes cluttered with useless unread e-mails, and offices cluttered with useless documents. Granted, creative personalities may thrive amid cluttered desks and crowded shelves, and staff should have the autonomy to customize their personal spaces as they see fit. However, excessive stimuli have been shown to decrease focus by overloading the senses and making it difficult for people to prioritize and focus on tasks (McMains and Kastner 2011, 587–97). Every unread e-mail or unsorted document represents a decision delayed or a task undone, every desktop notification is a distraction, and every search for a poorly named file is a waste of time. Results include frustration, anxiety, and reduced time and energy for leading innovation (Vozza 2015). Equally problematic is intellectual clutter—the mundane bureaucratic tasks like updating documentation or entering data into spreadsheets. Such tasks may be necessary but are also time and energy sucks. Libraries should work to streamline processes and sweep away clutter to free up brainpower and time—and money—for innovation.

Decluttering can quite literally create space for innovation. The author once cleared out a disused office, organizing or discarding boxes upon boxes of superseded documents, and then converted this cluttered storage space into a quiet space for intense creative thinking, for example, writing contracts or code. With seating and a portable whiteboard, the room is repurposable into an instant collaboration space or a private space for making telephone calls. Another decluttering project was to standardize file-naming conventions and purge redundant or unneeded documents from virtual file storage. Consequently, team members can locate needed materials immediately, saving time and frustration. Because of flexible spaces and organized data—easily restructured without a budget—library workers are free of mental clutter and can focus on innovating.

SAFE SPACES

Flexible spaces should be psychologically safe spaces. "In the best teams," Google researchers found, "members listen to one another and show sensitivity to feelings and needs" (Duhigg 2016). First and foremost, participants in innovation spaces must welcome one another regardless of other participants' race or ethnicity, sex, gender identity, or other traits and must ensure that all participants feel comfortable partaking in the conversations happening in those spaces. Second, leaders and team members alike must encourage honest, energetic, sensitive discussions and facilitate conversations to avoid disagreements turning personal. All participants in an innovation space should share ideas, and the group should consider those ideas thoughtfully and respectfully on their merits—and even if those ideas are found to be without merit, the fact that alternatives were proposed and entertained is symptomatic of a healthy organization open to disruption. If team members feel too psychologically unsafe to articulate "radical or risky ideas" or challenge others' ideas, then teams will not perform as effectively and innovation is doomed to falter (Sparrow 2010, 39–42).

Besides fostering psychologically safe collaborative environments, innovation spaces should support physically safe and healthy ergonomics that promote the well-being of workers. While plush chairs and couches in collaboration rooms are pleasant to have, ergonomics are vital to reducing muscular disorders, nervous strain, and resultant absenteeism while bolstering productivity and morale. Employers should provide readily customizable individual workstations and encourage workers to be proactive in evaluating and improving their individual and shared workspaces. Again, flexibility and choice are key. Standing desks, adjustable seating, softer lighting, ergonomically sound workstations with keyboards and mice positioned level with the elbows, and computer monitors positioned slightly below eye level to reduce neck strain—these are not mere perks. They foster productivity and support physical health and well-being, which in turn are strongly correlated with professional engagement and productivity (Bridger 2008; Gallup 2013, 50–52).

INNOVATION CULTURES

Of course, innovation spaces alone are insufficient to sustain engagement and innovation. Building intrapreneurial cultures is vital. Library leaders should tolerate risk, encourage creative thinking and change leadership by frontline staff, foster teamwork, and ensure that library-wide planning and resources align with areas of necessary innovation (Jantz 2012, 3–12). Library administrators are responsible for defining clear performance standards and holding individuals accountable for workmanship while fostering a sense of play—good humor, camaraderie, and imagination—in terms of ideas and projects (Sparrow 2010, 39–42). Creating innovation cultures forestalls the risk of innovation spaces being ineffective or misused, for example, the risk of serendipitous spaces becoming opportunities for counterproductive chit-chat and idleness. Libraries should recruit or allocate staff on the basis of entrepreneurial spirit and how they can support innovation in the organization as a whole, not strictly in the specialized positions they were hired to fill. The key takeaway for this section is that libraries should prioritize internal customer service: "the idea that the whole organization must serve those who serve" (Albrecht 1992, 101). Spaces are only one of many steps to foster innovation.

CONCLUSION

Innovation spaces for workers are an essential but often overlooked element of fostering intrapreneurial cultures in libraries and other organizations. For libraries of all types to survive and thrive, library leaders at all levels should prioritize creating or reconditioning workspaces to foster serendipity and collaboration, eliminate clutter, empower employees to adapt spaces to suit their needs and preferences, and ensure that all participants feel safe to express radical ideas and engage in vigorous discussions, while recognizing that not all workers are or need to be cutting-edge intrapreneurs. The locations of innovation spaces may be in library buildings or in virtual environments made possible by cloud-based wikis, communication and project management platforms, and other software that enables interactive virtual spaces. Equally, libraries should reasonably accommodate diverse needs and working styles and provide spaces for focused individual work as well as collaboration. Such spaces drive staff engagement and satisfaction and ultimately benefit end users without requiring massive infrastructure investments by libraries.

So, what can librarians do to make innovation spaces happen? Google, Steelcase, and other private-sector organizations provide models for successful and nuanced use of innovation spaces in the workplace, while libraries like NCSU have successfully adapted the tech industry's examples. Design consultants can analyze existing library spaces and staff and create blueprints for a redesign in which library administrators can invest. The point, however, is that library leaders at all levels can contribute to enhancing spaces. Any library worker can name files, shift furniture, or start conversations. Administrative funding and mandates for creating innovation spaces are vital, but the goal should be to foster innovations led by the workers themselves.

REFERENCES

Albrecht, Karl. 1992. *The Only Thing That Matters: Bringing the Power of the Customer into the Centre of Your Business*. New York: Harper.

Baregheh, Anahita, Jennifer Rowley, and Sally Sambrook. 2006. "Towards a Multidisciplinary Definition of Innovation." *Management Decision* 47 (8): 1324. doi:10.1108/00251740910984578.

Berry, John N., III. 2007. "Great Work, Genuine Problems." *Library Journal* 132 (16): 26–29.

Bloom, Louise, and Romily Faulkner. 2016. "Innovation Spaces: Lessons from the United Nations." *Third World Quarterly* 37 (8): 1371–87. doi:10.1080/01436597.2015.1135730.

Bostick, Sharon L., and Brian Irwin. 2015. "Changing Spaces: Creating the Next Generation of Work Environments for Library Staff." *Proceedings of the IATUL Conferences*. http://docs.lib.purdue.edu/iatul/2015/cel/3.

Bridger, R. S. 2008. *Introduction to Ergonomics*. 3rd ed. Boca Raton, Fla.: CRC Press.

Cain, Susan. 2012. *Quiet: The Power of Introverts in a World That Can't Stop Talking*. New York: Crown.

Castree, Noel, Rob Kitchin, and Alisdair Rogers. 2013. "Innovation." In *A Dictionary of Human Geography*. Oxford: Oxford University Press.

de Jong, Jeroen, and Sander Wennekers. 2008. *Intrapreneurship: Conceptualizing Entrepreneurial Employee Behaviour*. Zoetermeer, Netherlands: SCALES.

Drucker, Peter F. 2003. *A Functioning Society: Community, Society, and Polity in the Twentieth Century*. New Brunswick, N.J.: Transaction.

Duhigg, Charles. 2016. "What Google Learned from Its Quest to Build the Perfect Team." *New York Times Magazine*, February 25. http://www.nytimes.com/2016/02/28/magazine/what-google-learned-from-its-quest-to-build-the-perfect-team.html.

Felício, J. Augusto, Ricardo Rodrigues, and Vítor R Caldeirinha. 2012. "The Effect of Intrapreneurship on Corporate Performance." *Management Decision* 50 (10): 1717–38. doi:10.1108/00251741211279567.

Felix, Elliot. 2015. "Rethink the Staff Workplace." *Library Journal*, May 28. http://lj.libraryjournal.com/2015/05/buildings/lbd/rethink-the-staff-workplace-library-by-design-spring-2015/.

Gallup. 2013. *State of the American Workplace: Employee Engagement Insights for U.S. Business Leaders*. Washington, D.C.: Gallup. Accessed 2016. http://employeeengagement.com/wp-content/uploads/2013/06/Gallup-2013-State-of-the-American-Workplace-Report.pdf.

Goldenson, Jeff, and Nate Hill. 2013. "Making Room for Innovation." *Library Journal*, May 16. http://lj.libraryjournal.com/2013/05/future-of-libraries/making-room-for-innovation/.

Jantz, Ronald C. 2012. "Innovation in Academic Libraries: An Analysis of University Librarians' Perspectives." *Library & Information Science Research* 34: 3–12. doi:10.1016/j.lisr.2011.07.008.

Kristal, Marc. 2014. "Quest for Quiet." *Metropolis Magazine*, June. http://www.metropolismag.com/June-2014/Quest-for-Quiet/.

Largo-Wight, Erin, W. William Chen, Virginia Dodd, and Robert Weiler. 2011. "Healthy Workplaces: The Effects of Nature Contact at Work on Employee Stress and Health." *Public Health Reports* 126, Supplement 1: 124–30.

Manley, Will. 2011. "My Professional Heroes: Let's Hear It for the Front-Line Grunts Who Make Service Happen." *American Libraries*, April 27. https://americanlibrariesmagazine.org/2011/04/27/my-professional-heroes/.

McMains, Stephanie, and Sabine Kastner. 2011. "Interactions of Top-Down and Bottom-Up Mechanisms in Human Visual Cortex." *Journal of Neuroscience* 31 (2): 587–97. doi:10.1523/JNEUROSCI.3766-10.2011.

Molaro, Antony. 2013. "What Librarians Lack: The Importance of the Entrepreneurial Spirit." *Information Activist* (blog), June 17. https://informationactivist.com/2013/06/17/what-librarians-lack-the-importance-of-the-entrepreneurial-spirit/.

Morris, Meredith Ringel, Andrew Begel, and Ben Wiedermann. 2015. "Understanding the Challenges Faced by Neurodiverse Software Engineering Employees: Towards a More Inclusive and Productive Technical Workforce." In *ASSETS '15: Proceedings of the 17th International ACM SIGACCESS Conference on Computers & Accessibility*, Lisbon, Portugal, October 26–28, 2015, 177, 180. New York: ACM. doi:10.1145/2700648.2809841.

North Carolina State University. 2008. *James B. Hunt Jr. Library Programming & Pre-design: Final Report.* Last modified October 24, 2008. https://www.lib.ncsu.edu/sites/default/files/huntlibrary/documents/102508_ppd.pdf.

Scherdin, Mary Jane, and Anne K. Beaubien. 1995. "Shattering Our Stereotype: Librarians' New Image." *Library Journal* 120 (12): 35–38.

Silverman, Rachel Emma. 2013. "The Science of Serendipity in the Workplace." *Wall Street Journal*, April 30. http://on.wsj.com/1024bc8.

Sparrow, Paul. 2010. "Cultures of Innovation." *Human Resources*, 39–42.

Spinuzzi, Clay. 2003. *Tracing Genres through Organizations: A Sociocultural Approach to Information Design.* Cambridge, Mass.: MIT Press.

Stewart, James B. 2013. "Looking for a Lesson in Google's Perks." *New York Times*, March 15. http://www.nytimes.com/2013/03/16/business/at-google-a-place-to-work-and-play.html.

Swanbrow, Diane. 2012. "Sharing Space: Proximity Breeds Collaboration." *University of Michigan News*, October 25. http://www.ns.umich.edu/new/releases/20932-sharing-space-proximity-breeds-collaboration.

Vozza, Stephanie. 2015. "7 Ways Clutter Is Ruining Your Life." *Fast Company*, November 9. https://www.fastcompany.com/3052894/how-to-be-a-success-at-everything/7-ways-clutter-is-ruining-your-life.

Part III

Technology

Chapter Seven

The Promise and Perils of Open Source

Junior Tidal

Libraries have adopted open source software (OSS) for a variety of projects throughout the years. This chapter is an examination of these endeavors. It will define OSS, review current literature of open source technologies in use, examine library-related software and hardware programs, look into the distribution of the open source software, and showcase the author's personal experience in experimenting with open source web content management systems (CMSs). This includes the inherent value and benefits of using OSS as well as the obscure costs and challenges in deploying them.

WHAT IS OPEN SOURCE SOFTWARE (OSS)?

OSS is computer software where the program's source code is freely accessible. Anyone, from users to developers, can look at how the code of a software program works. Software can be downloaded and installed to be used at no cost. It may also be necessary to download supplemental OSS software in order for it to run. It is "free" in the sense where the code is not restricted and programmers can alter how it works by altering, amending, or deleting portions of the code. There are a number of licenses available that dictate the distribution of code, attribution, and derivative works. According to the Open Source Initiative, many of these licenses follow the definition of open source (https://opensource.org/licenses) ("Licenses and Standards" 2016). Andrew St. Laurent (2004, 4) states that the purpose of open source licensing is to deny the "right to exclusively exploit a work." Even further, the definition of OSS itself explicitly states that the license cannot discriminate against particular persons or fields or endeavors. Open source, with this in mind, goes just beyond source code and has become a philosophy.

There is an apparent synergy between open source and the values of librarianship. Firstly, the idea of information being freely available fits well with the very definition of open source. Access to the inner workings of OSS is akin to the unfettered information that libraries store and provide. Community-driven collaboration is highly valued among librarians and open source developers (Puckett 2012). Privacy and transparency are also championed between librarians and the OSS community.

OSS promotes innovation. Since the code is freely available, it can be modified, and distributed for use in other projects. Reusing existing code integrates functionality faster, works well with time limits and resource confinement, and helps save on costs (Haefliger, von Krogh, and Spaeth 2008, 193). OSS can also facilitate evolution, as it is continually improved so long as there is a community that supports and uses it. Since code is freely shared, OSS facilitates remote and local collaboration in development (Yamauchi et al. 2000, 329–38). This has since been recognized by a number of companies. Microsoft has made their popular .NET framework more open to entice developers in the hopes of community-driven coding (Krill 2016). Facebook has also launched open source projects to contribute to the larger community as well as enhance the company's reputation among developers for recruitment. Google has also contributed to many open source projects (Assay 2009), and has opened the code of TensorFlow, its artificial intelligence engine (Metz 2015), as well.

Multiple OSS products can also be used in tandem to solve a common problem. Popular OSS tools among libraries—including VuFind, a replacement for the traditional OPAC; Koha, an integrated library system; and DSpace, an institutional repository—have been used together to provide functionality that only one alone could not provide (Balnaves 2013). Later in this chapter, these tools and their functions will be further explored.

Proprietary software, on the other hand, can be considered "closed" software. Code is not available for modification or redistribution. Unlike the OSS model, closed software increases costs for libraries. This can include not only purchasing the software but implementation and support as well (Coombs and Hollister 2014, 4). Libraries are locked into particular vendors for their services, which may include subscription fees that are subject to increases. Some library systems may also require users to utilize specific components available only through a particular vendor. There could potentially be other costs, such as fees to migrate, maintain, or upgrade data between older and newer systems. However, these economic factors impact whether a library should choose between proprietary and OSS solutions.

Other "open" movements that libraries have favored have been greatly influenced by OSS. The distribution model of OSS has made an impact on the open access/open educational resources (OER) movement. This is evident in the Budapest Open Access Initiative, a public statement that advocates readers of open access text be able to "read, download, copy, distribute, print, search, or link to the full texts of these articles, crawl them for indexing, pass them as data to software, or use them for any other lawful purpose, without financial, legal, or technical barriers other than those inseparable from gaining access to the internet itself" (Chan et al. 2002). This sentiment reflects the tenets of sharing open source code. For example, if you replace the word "texts" with software code, it would imitate an open source license. The open source textbook model supports collaboration and development methods that mirror OSS. This model frees authors from the constraints of publishers (Bergman 2014, 10) as much as open source frees coders from software companies. The open hardware movement has also been directly influenced by OSS. Not only is open hardware the foundation of makerspaces made popular by libraries, the devices created through open hardware initiatives have been used to collect data on libraries' physical space (Yuvaraj and Maurya 2016).

LITERATURE REVIEW

Richard Stallman, activist and founder of the free software movement, said it best, stating that "open source software is not unlike some of the basic principles of librarianship in America" (Stallman, quoted in Morgan 2002, 12). The OSS movement mirrors the ethical values of librarians, where information is freely shared for the common good (Puckett 2012). Public, academic, special, and rural libraries have adopted OSS. In 2014, an Association of Research Libraries SPEC survey noted that out of seventy-six member institutions, 97 percent have adopted OSS (Thacker, Knutson, and Dehmlow 2014). Not only have libraries embraced OSS development, but its use has been widely researched and written about. From 2001 through 2012, there have been 156 articles written specifically about libraries and their implementation of OSS (Palmer and Choi 2014, 11–27).

There are a number of reasons why libraries would use OSS solutions. The most obvious reason is cost. Libraries have adopted OSS due to its free or low barrier of economic implementation, and ease of evaluation (code can be easily acquired, installed, used, and assessed) (Corrado 2005). OSS is appealing to librarians due to "the freedom, flexibility, customization, and lower cost that it promises" (Singh 2014b). Prohibitive costs can also be the catalyst that drives OSS in libraries. Libki, a kiosk-based public computer sign-up system, was developed because the rural library system using it could not afford a proprietary solution (Hall, Ames, and Brice 2013). The Koha integrated library system (ILS) was selected because it was the most cost effective for the Royal London Homoeopathic Hospital compared to its proprietary counterparts (Bissels 2008, 303–14). Although propriety software is heavily used in libraries, they can easily be locked in to a particular vendor or company. If that vendor goes out of business or decides not to support its software, then the library has little control on what to do (Corrado 2005). Additionally, vendors have become more consolidated as they have purchased and absorbed one another, creating "higher stakes for libraries" (Breeding 2016b).

There are also other benefits in implementing and developing OSS for libraries. Librarians learn about software development. James Corbly (2014, 65) argues that OSS makes librarians better, improving time management skills, making better use of their resources, and improving customer service across the organization. As the library profession has increasingly become more network and computer oriented, it has forced librarians to increase their own digital literacy. Librarians may need to install or learn about software or hardware outside of the scope of the initial OSS project. This may require more planning than simply downloading a program and running it.

The other strength of OSS is that it is customizable. If the staff has the expertise, OSS can be specifically tailored for the needs of a library and its users. Adopting OSS has also attributed to better relationships between libraries and community stakeholders, as well as partnership libraries pooling their resources for projects (Mehra, Singh, and Parris 2010, 690–701). However, libraries in particular do not typically contribute to the development of OSS projects, despite being proponents of them (Askey 2008).

Libraries can retrieve OSS-based software from a variety of places. GitHub (https://github.com), a repository of open source projects, has been the emergent platform to share code (Thacker and Knutson 2015). Many developers and academic libraries have freely shared code using this system, including the New York Public Library, Digital Public Library of America, Library of Congress, Stanford University Libraries, and North Carolina State University Libraries. GitHub also promotes remote and local collaboration, as developers can clone others' work, modify it, and redistribute it through development branches of the original project. Robin Camille Davis (2015, 158–64) notes that not only can GitHub be used to share code, it is also a social network for developers that can facilitate collaborative scholarly writing and be used to track digital archiving.

Numerous OSS projects can also be found on FOSS4lib.org. What originally began on the OSS4lib e-mail Listserv by Dan Chudnov, FOSS4lib.org is a site that provides a listing of library-based OSS projects. The site is partially funded by an Andrew W. Mellon Foundation grant and a partnership with the nonprofit organization LYRASIS.

With the existence of these online distribution points, there comes the problem of choosing which OSS project to use. Some libraries form internal research teams to consult with developers, vendors, scholarly journals, conferences, and professional contacts (Singh 2013, 206–19). The aforementioned FOSS4lib.org site offers rubrics to assist librarians in selecting which OSS project is best for them. Rubrics were used in selecting a discovery layer for Indiana University (Moore and Greene 2012, 24–30) as well, selecting the electronic resource management system CORAL for the Fenway Library Consortium (Drake et al. 2014). A rubric is also used when OSS projects specific for libraries are vetted through an informal review process by library and information science (LIS) professionals (Sarma 2016). Ohio State University used an in-depth study of workflows and an analysis of the total cost of ownership in evaluating the adoption of the electronic peer-review publishing systems Open Journal System and DPubS (Samuels and Griffy 2012, 41–62).

BARRIERS TO THE ADOPTION OF OSS

Despite the promises of OSS, there are a number of barriers that prevent libraries from utilizing them. Igor Steinmacher et al. (2015, 67–85) outline various factors that prohibit the adoption of OSS, including the lack of socialization, the high technological skill necessary to maintain an open source project, and poor documentation. Open source also comes with "hidden costs." Just because it is free, doesn't necessarily mean there are no expenditures. The biggest cost is the labor of support, expertise, implementation, and customization for libraries (Corbly 2014, 65). Programmers may be needed to oversee an OSS project, which may also require new staffing or open positions. Some libraries may also depend on a separate IT organization such as a campus office for academic institutions or a city IT department for public libraries. This may cause a library to lose control of an OSS project (Jost 2015, 53). Even though an open source license supports inclusivity of users, Bret Davidson and Jason Casden (2016) note that OSS favors well-funded institution and developer communities rather than diverse ones. Perhaps this is due to the staffing and expertise that is typically found in larger institutions, lack of technical expertise in smaller ones, or a combination of both.

The lack of technical support has also been a barrier in adopting OSS solutions. Technical issues regarding OSS are especially challenging to libraries, either while evaluating or adopting them (Singh 2014a, 688–709). Regardless, librarians should be willing to experiment with OSS. Peter Fernandez (2012) argues that institutions should acknowledge if an OSS project meets the needs of its patrons, within the context of the software's cost, the mission of the institution, and the value of a sustainable public good. Kyle Hall, Cindy Murdock Ames, and John Brice (2013) state that a "willingness to think in nontraditional ways and full management backing" is needed to develop OSS projects. There have also been strides in providing more than just user-based community support for library OSS projects. Open source library vendors provide training and support for systems such as Koha (Jost 2015). Nonprofits who have taken a role in governing open source projects have become instrumental in providing support, migration, and even custom development, all within the scope of open source licensing (Breeding 2016c, 1). Library associations, such as the Librarians Registration Council of Nigeria, have also held workshops to assist with the training of widespread OSS tools for underfunded institutions (Oweh 2014). Library vendors are also taking notice of the power of open source. EBSCO is funding an open source, collaborative library services platform in developing a discovery tool (Breeding 2016a). Known as FOLIO, or the future of libraries, it is a collaboration between EBSCO, libraries, and other vendors to create extensible resource management tools (http://folio.org).

LIBRARY OSS PROJECTS

Libraries all over the world are utilizing many open source solutions to enhance their institutions. In 2006, Chudnov outlined a number of OSS programs available for libraries that ranged from bibliographic management tools, OPACS, and repositories (Chudnov 2007, 21). Today, the number of OSS programs available for libraries has greatly increased, covering many different aspects of librarianship. The next section explores the various OSS tools available specifically for libraries. Although this is not an exhaustive list, it may be useful for those who are considering OSS alternatives for traditional library technologies.

Digital Libraries and Institutional Repositories

Digital libraries and institutional repositories use many open source software packages. A digital library is typically a collection of digital objects curated under a specific set of standards. Institutional repositories are archives that collect the digital output of an institution and that of its community members, accessible online. Dion Hoe-Lian Goh et al. (2006, 360–79) developed a twelve-point checklist to evaluate different OSS software packages for digital libraries. The top evaluated software is Greenstone (http://www. greenstone.org/), which is an open source digital library platform that manages and displays information systems (Witten et al. 2000, 113–21). Other systems such as DSpace, Fedora Commons, EPrints, and Invenio have also been evaluated. Depending on the type of digital collection they are curating, libraries can choose either an "out of the box" or expertise-required OSS digital library solution (Pyrounakis, Nikolaidou, and Hatzopoulos 2014, 13).

The Hydra Project (https://projecthydra.org/) is a framework for a digital repository, built on open source applications. It began as a multi-institutional community effort, including University of Virginia, University of Hull, and Stanford University. It now has more than thirty institutional partners, including Columbia University, the Digital Public Library of America, WGBH, the Rock and Roll Hall of Fame, Indiana University, and Yale University to name a few. It can be used to support image collections, media libraries, and archives.

Integrated Library Systems (ILS)

Evergreen (https://evergreen-ils.org) is a GNU GPL licensed ILS that is used by more than 1,800 libraries worldwide. Developed by the Georgia Public Library System in 2006, it manages circulation transactions, library automation, acquisitions, and the capability to share resources (Albee and Chen 2014, 391). Evergreen (and Koha) has been evaluated using a ten-point system based on the expectations of a "Next Generation Library Catalog" (Yang and Hofmann 2010, 141). The project is supported through open source vendors, mailing lists, Internet chat, and community blog posts.

Koha (http://koha.org) was developed by Chris Cormack in 1999. It is an ILS initially created to connect branches with a central library. Widely used among library professionals (Macan, Fernández, and Stojanovski 2013, 141), it utilizes circulation, patron management, serials, and cataloging modules. Tristan Müller (2011, 77) notes that Koha is the most complete ILS, due to the many features that it possesses. Utilized by a large user base, it has been under consistent and continual improvement since its launch.

Kuali Open Library Environment (OLE) (http://www.kuali.org/ole/) began in 2008. The directive of the project is "to build an enterprise-level, open-source, and next-generation ILS" (Wang and Dawes 2012, 76). It is built through a partnership of higher education institutions, including Cornell University, Duke University, EBSCO, Indiana University, Chicago University, and many others, and funded through an Andrew W. Mellon grant. It contains four modules that facilitate an ILS: Select & Acquire (acquisitions), Describe & Manage (cataloging), Systems Integration (authentication), and Deliver (circulation). It is supported through user groups and an e-mail Listserv. Marshall Breeding (2016a) mentions that the enthusiasm and widespread adoption of Kuali built the foundation of EBSCO's FOLIO project.

Discovery Tools

Blacklight, also known as Project Blacklight (http://projectblacklight.org/), is a discovery tool layer developed by the University of Virginia Library (see figure 7.1). It is used by many institutions, including Johns Hopkins University, Stanford University, Indiana University, and WGBH, Boston's public broadcasting station (Moore and Greene 2012, 26). It contains numerous features, such as facet searching, relevance ranking, and specific customization. Its underlying structure utilizes Apache Solr, the open source indexing engine, and is written in Ruby on Rails.

Developed by two librarians at the Miami University Libraries, SolrPAC (http://beta.lib.muohio.edu/) is a Drupal module that can facilitate catalog searching. Ross Shanely-Roberts and Rob Casson, respectively a systems librarian and a cataloger, built SolrPAC without any formal computer science training (Lomker et al. 2009, 234). Similar to the other discovery tools above, SolrPAC is powered by Apache Solr. It uses the open source Drupal content management system (CMS) to display content. It is written in PHP, highly customizable, and utilizes tagging and faceted searches.

VuFind (http://vufind-org.github.io/vufind/) is a library resource portal and scrapes data from OPACs, institutional repositories, and other sources through a single Google-like search box (Denton and Coysh 2011, 301–19). It is created and maintained by Villanova University. This project is coded in PHP and, like Blacklight, utilizes Apache Solr to index its records. VuFind also uses faceted searching and various criteria to sort search results.

Web Applications

Developed in 2010, CORAL (http://coral-erm.org/) is an electronic resource management system (ERMS) used to organize libraries' article, journal, and media databases (see figure 7.2). Robin Malott and Benjamin Heet of the University of Notre Dame developed Centralized Online Resources Acquisitions and Licensing due to the prohibitive costs of propriety solutions (Whit-

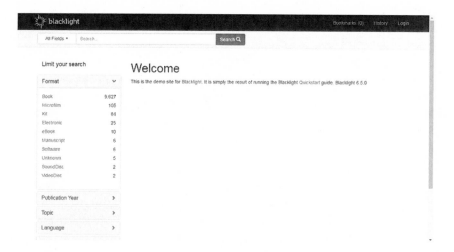

Figure 7.1.   Project Blacklight is an open source discovery tool.

field 2011, 19) and to improve the workflow of managing resources (Elguindi and Schmidt 2012, 49). Libraries can manage electronic resources, including URLs, licensing information, and usage statistics, all from the comfort of their web browser. It is used for its flexibility and adaptability for a number of institutions, including Texas A&M University, Southern Illinois University at Carbondale, and Wake Forest University (Imre, Hartnett, and Hiatt 2013, 224–34).

Guide on the Side (http://code.library.arizona.edu/) is a web application used to build online tutorials within the browser. Developers at the University of Arizona wrote the program using PHP and MySQL. It is touted for having a small learning curve. If users can operate Microsoft Word, they can utilize Guide on the Side due to the similarity in the interface. Users are supported by an active Google Group and a GitHub issue queue (Schmidt and Hartman 2015, 163).

OpenRoom (https://www.bsu.edu/libraries/getopenroom/) is a PHP-based room reservation system. Built from the remnants of OpenScheduler, Ball State University developed an open source room reservation system specifically for their needs (Faust, Hafner, and Seaton 2010). It was developed out of necessity, due to the lack of existing proprietary solutions. The application was also a move away from a paper-based system, enhancing the workflow involved in reserving rooms.

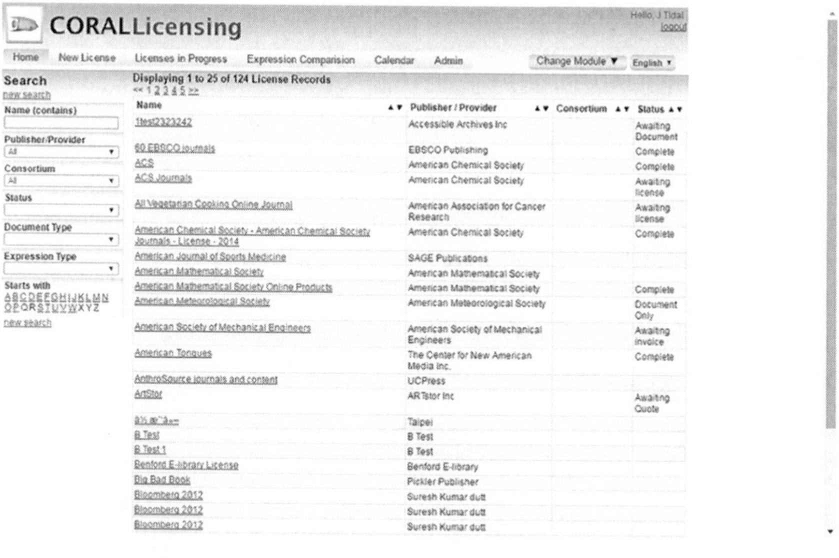

Figure 7.2. CORAL is an open source electronic resource management system.

SubjectsPlus (http://www.subjectsplus.com/) is a content management system used to organize research guides. Written by Andrew Darby of Ithaca College, it can be used to manage electronic databases, research guides, and a staff directory. Written in PHP and powered by MySQL, it was derived from an abandoned open source application called PirateSource. Darby developed and improved the program after retrieving permission from East Carolina University, and in open source fashion, relicensed and redistributed the program (Corrado and Frederick 2008). It has been adopted by a number of libraries, including Wichita State University Libraries, due to its low cost and ease of use among librarians of various technical skills (Blackburn and Walker 2010).

Zotero (https://www.zotero.org/) is a bibliographic citation tool. Funded by grants and led by developers at George Mason University (Cohen 2008), this online web tool assists users with organizing citation information. The program can be downloaded as a plug-in for the Mozilla Firefox browser or as a desktop client. The desktop client can interact with either Google's Chrome browser or Apple Safari. Zotero detects and scrapes citation information when a user is on a web page. Users can tag, sort, or annotate citations. It is a useful open source tool that can empower library users (Ritterbush 2007, 111–22). Zotero also encourages users to connect with one another in pursuing similar research (Cohen 2008).

Other Library OSS Projects

Libki (http://libki.org/) is a library kiosk program developed by the Crawford County Federated Library System (CCFLS) in Pennsylvania. It is used to manage the reservation of public computers in libraries using a web-based interface compatible with Windows or Linux systems. The project took more than five hundred hours of development and three different versions, yet has saved the CCFLS hundreds of dollars, with implementations in one academic and five public libraries (Hall, Ames, and Brice 2013).

THE PERILS OF OPEN SOURCE

My personal experience with OSS focuses mainly on web development for an academic library. Some of these projects were failures, yet learning experiences, while others have been more successful. This includes the content management systems PHP Nuke, Joomla, Drupal, WordPress, and MediaWiki.

In 2008, the New York City College of Technology's (City Tech) Ursula C. Schwerin Library web server had migrated from a shared Windows IIS server to a dedicated LAMP stack. A LAMP stack is a commonly used web server configuration that consists of the following OSS: Linux, Apache,

MySQL, and PHP. Each of these components is freely available. Support was purchased for the Linux distribution, Redhat Enterprise, which was the chosen operating system for the server. Apache serves web pages. MySQL, a database programming language, stored content, and PHP, or Hypertext Pre-processor, is a scripting language to code dynamic web pages. MySQL and PHP are common requirements for content management systems.

The content management systems that were considered to power the library's web server included PHP Nuke, Joomla, Drupal, and WordPress. PHP Nuke (https://www.phpnuke.org/) was initially evaluated as the library's CMS. It is, hence the namesake, a PHP-based CMS. It contains numerous modules that would be useful for a library website, including a calendar, file management, and a staff directory. However, due to security concerns, it was abandoned. Although the program was consistently patched with security updates, it was susceptible to MySQL injection scripts, which can disable the site.

Joomla (https://www.joomla.org/) was also tested as a CMS for the library's website. It is widely used and contains a number of modules and plug-ins that would be useful for a library website. However, at the same time, the back end suffers from a steep learning curve. Some librarians felt it was not intuitive enough to use. The early version of Joomla required numerous clicks to alter or add content. It was also prone to spam user accounts. This, too, was not a proper fit for the City Tech Library.

The popular blog platform WordPress (https://www.wordpress.org) was also considered to be used as a CMS for the library website. However, after some testing, it seemed the platform was best used for blogging rather than managing a library website. Firstly, it is well known for security vulnerabilities and constant updating. The search functionality is limited, and although it boasts numerous plug-ins, these plug-ins can conflict with one another and can cause errors. Despite these drawbacks, the library decided to keep Word-Press not only as a blog, but it was also adopted to be used as a subsite for freshman orientation, the library newsletter, and a staff intranet.

Finally, in 2009, the Drupal CMS was adopted, using the sixth version of the program. Since then, we have upgraded to Drupal 7 and, as of this writing, the CMS is up to its eighth version. One of the reasons it was selected was its wide popularity among libraries. A list of libraries utilizing Drupal can be found on the Drupal Groups Libraries page (https://groups. drupal.org/libraries/libraries). Additionally, there is a Library Information Technology Association (LITA) interest group and a dedicated Listserv (DRUPAL4LIB). For our needs, Drupal has been used to power our desktop website, a separate mobile site, and the current responsively designed website. The system was also selected for its numerous features, such as user administration, in-browser editing, taxonomy management, and its most powerful resource, the modules that it offers. These user-created modules can be used to establish custom content types, from e-resources to library events, which can be filtered and presented to the user.

Although Drupal has powered our website for more than seven years, it has not been a seamless transition from our home-brewed PHP-based CMS. Firstly, Drupal's strength lies in its community created modules. These modules are used to augment Drupal. Modules can be used for many functions essential for library websites, such as managing electronic databases (Klein 2008), aggregating blog posts and calendar RSS feeds, or processing forms. However, utilizing these modules takes a lot of experimentation. Some modules are incompatible with others, where at best, the module doesn't work and at worst, it crashes the whole site. Although there is a huge Drupal user and developer base that works directly with libraries, such as online groups, Listservs, and conferences, there may not be support when utilizing multiple modules. Using OSS is accepting the risks of having sporadic or even unavailable support, especially for emerging or less-known technologies.

Configurations differ among Drupal-powered library websites. Different versions of PHP and Apache can cause havoc for some modules. This may require either modifications to the module itself or adopting alternative versions. This requires constant troubleshooting and testing to make sure that a site works. It is also a good reason to utilize a test server when experimenting with Drupal. This can be said for any OSS project, if funds and expertise are available to do so.

Upgrading Drupal can also be a challenge. Minor upgrades require the site to be taken offline, and major upgrades aren't always seamless. As in the case of any upgrade, Drupal requires file and database backups in case of any hiccups. Like WordPress, Drupal is also susceptible to hacking, which prompts for frequent security patches and updates.

CONCLUSION

OSS provides free, cost-effective technological solutions for libraries. However, maintaining their sustainability requires the willingness to experiment and take risks of institutional administrators. Maha Shaikh and Tony Cornford created a conceptual model known as TCO, or total cost of ownership, which is used to analyze the cost of identifying, acquiring, installing, operating, and discontinuing the use of OSS (Shaikh and Cornford 2011, 60). TCO helps place the adoption of OSS in not just financial terms, but their impact on an organization's exiting technology infrastructure, values, culture, and strategic goals.

Implementing OSS seems more applicable than ever regarding the current economic climate. As libraries have tighter budget constraints, OSS has become almost a necessity for the modern-day library. In some cases of the development of OSS programs, they were birthed from such economic conditions. The return of investment on OSS is greater control over services and less dependence on external library interests.

REFERENCES

Albee, Barbara, and Hsin-liang Chen. 2014. "Public Library Staff's Perceived Value and Satisfaction of an Open Source Library System." *Electronic Library* 32 (3): 390–402.

Askey, Dale. 2008. "We Love Open Source Software. No, You Can't Have Our Code." *code4lib Journal* 5.

Assay, Matt. 2009. "World's Biggest Open-Source Company? Google." CNET. September 16. http://www.cnet.com/news/worlds-biggest-open-source-company-google/.

Balnaves, Edmund. 2013. "From OPAC to Archive: Integrated Discovery and Digital Libraries with Open Source." Paper presented at IFLA WLIC, Singapore.

Bergman, Seth D. 2014. "Open Source Textbooks: A Paradigm Derived from Open Source Software." *Publishing Research Quarterly* 30 (1): 10.

Bissels, Gerhard. 2008. "Implementation of an Open Source Library Management System: Experiences with Koha 3.0 at the Royal London Homoeopathic Hospital." *Program* 42 (3): 303–14.

Blackburn, Gemma, and Mary Walker. 2010. "Subject Guides & More: Creatively Transforming an Open Source Management System." *code4Lib Journal* 12.

Breeding, Marshall. 2016a. "EBSCO Supports New Open Source Project." *American Libraries Magazine*, April 22. Accessed August 25, 2016. https://americanlibrariesmagazine.org/2016/04/22/ebsco-kuali-open-source-project/.

———. 2016b. "Library Systems Report 2016." *American Libraries Magazine*, May 2. Accessed August 24, 2016. https://americanlibrariesmagazine.org/2016/05/02/library-systems-report-2016/.

———. 2016c. "Smarter Libraries through Technology: Library Technology via Nonprofits." *Smart Libraries Newsletter* 36 (1): 1.

Chan, Leslie, Darius Cuplinskas, Michael Eisen, Fred Friend, Yana Genova, Jean-Claude Guédon, Melissa Hagemann, et al. 2002. *Budapest Open Access Initiative*. http://www.budapestopenaccessinitiative.org/read.

Chudnov, Dan. 2007. "The Future of FLOSS in Libraries." In *Information Tomorrow: Reflections on Technology and the Future of Public and Academic Libraries*, edited by Rachel S. Gordon, 19–30. Medford, N.J.: Information Today.

Cohen, Daniel J. 2008. "Creating Scholarly Tools and Resources for the Digital Ecosystem: Building Connections in the Zotero Project." *First Monday* 13 (8).

Coombs, Karen A., and Amanda J. Hollister. 2014. *Open Source Web Applications for Libraries*. Medford, N.J.: Information Today.

Corbly, James E. 2014. "The Free Software Alternative: Freeware, Open-Source Software, and Libraries." *Information Technology and Libraries* 33 (3): 65.

Corrado, Edward M. 2005. "The Importance of Open Access, Open Source, and Open Standards for Libraries." *Issues in Science and Technology Librarianship* 42 (1092–1206).

Corrado, Edward M., and Kathryn A. Frederick. 2008. "Free and Open Source Options for Creating Database-Driven Subject Guides." *code4Lib Journal* 2 (9).

Davidson, Bret, and Jason Casden. 2016. "Beyond Open Source: Evaluating the Community Availability of Software." *code4Lib Journal* 31.

Davis, Robin Camille. 2015. "Git and GitHub for Librarians." *Behavioral & Social Sciences Librarian* 34 (3): 158–64.

Denton, William, and Sarah J. Coysh. 2011. "Usability Testing of VuFind at an Academic Library." *Library Hi Tech* 29 (2): 301–19.

Drake, Kelly, Marilyn Geller, Erin Wentz, and Louisa Choy. 2014. *When the Open Source System Is the Best System*. LYRASYS. (PDF e-book). https://discuss.foss4lib.org/sites/default/files/inline/When%20the%20Open%20Source%20System%20is%20the%20

Best%20Sy%20%20Kelly%20Drake%2C%20Marilyn%20Geller%2C%20Erin%20Wentz %2C%20Louisa%20Choy.pdf.

Elguindi, Anne C., and Kari Schmidt. 2012. *Electronic Resource Management: Practical Perspectives in a New Technical Services Model*. Oxford: Chandos.

Faust, Bradley D., Arthur W. Hafner, and Robert L. Seaton. 2010. "OpenRoom: Making Room Reservation Easy for Students and Faculty." *code4Lib Journal* 10.

Fernandez, Peter. 2012. "Library Values That Interface with Technology: Public Service Information Professionals, Zotero, and Open Source Software Decision Making." *Library Philosophy and Practice*. http://digitalcommons.unl.edu/cgi/viewcontent.cgi?article=1992& context=libphilprac.

Goh, Dion Hoe-Lian, Alton Chua, Davina Anqi Khoo, Emily Boon-Hui Khoo, Eric Bok-Tong Mak, and Maple Wen-Min Ng. 2006. "A Checklist for Evaluating Open Source Digital Library Software." *Online Information Review* 30 (4): 360–79.

Haefliger, Stefan, Georg von Krogh, and Sebastian Spaeth. 2008. "Code Reuse in Open Source Software." *Management Science* 54 (1): 193.

Hall, Kyle, Cindy Murdock Ames, and John Brice. 2013. "Open Source Library Software Development in a Small Rural Library System." *code4Lib Journal* 19.

Imre, Andrea, Eric Hartnett, and C. Derrik Hiatt. 2013. "CORAL: Implementing an Open-Source ERM System." *Serials Librarian* 64 (1–4): 224–34.

Jost, Richard. 2015. *Selecting and Implementing an Integrated Library System: The Most Important Decision You Will Ever Make*. Waltham, Mass.: Chandos.

Klein, Leo. 2008. "Screencast: Creating a Library Database Page with Drupal." *Chicago Librarian* (blog). February 19. http://chicagolibrarian.com/node/262.

Krill, Paul. 2016. "Microsoft Will Deliver Open Source .Net Core in June." *InfoWorld*, May 10. http://www.infoworld.com/article/3068572/microsoft-windows/microsoft-will-deliver-open-source-net-core-in-june.html.

"Licenses and Standards." 2016. Open Source Initiative. Accessed June 1, 2016. https:// opensource.org/licenses.

Lomker, Linda Haack, Sharon Shafer, Marlena Frackowski, Dustin Larmore, and Richard Wayne. 2009. "Technical Services Report." *Technical Services Quarterly* 26 (3): 234. doi:10.1080/07317130802520310.

Macan, Bojan, Gladys Vanesa Fernández, and Jadranka Stojanovski. 2013. "Open Source Solutions for Libraries: ABCD vs. Koha." *Program* 47 (2): 136–54.

Mehra, Bharat, Vandana Singh, and Hannah Parris. 2010. "Open Source Software Collaborations in Tennessee's Regional Library System: An Exploratory Study." *Library Review* 59 (9): 690–701.

Metz, Cade. 2015. "Google Just Open Sourced TensorFlow, Its Artificial Intelligence Engine." Wired, November 9. http://www.wired.com/2015/11/google-open-sources-its-artificial-intelligence-engine/.

Moore, Kate B., and Courtney Greene. 2012. "The Search for a New OPAC: Selecting an Open Source Discovery Layer." *Serials Review* 38, (1): 24–30.

Morgan, Eric. 2002. "Possibilities for Open Source Software in Libraries." *Information Technology and Libraries* 21 (1): 12.

Müller, Tristan. 2011. "How to Choose a Free and Open Source Integrated Library System." *OCLC Systems & Services: International Digital Library Perspectives* 27 (1): 77.

Oweh, Innocent. 2014. "Librarian Council, NITDA Train Professionals in Open Source Software Application." *Africa News Service*, August 13.

Palmer, Aaron, and Namjoo Choi. 2014. "The Current State of Library Open Source Software Research." *Library Hi Tech* 32 (1): 11–27. doi:10.1108/lht-05-2013-0056.

Puckett, Jason. 2012. "Open Source Software and Librarian Values." *Georgia Library Quarterly* 49 (3): Article 9. http://digitalcommons.kennesaw.edu/glq/vol49/iss3/9.

Pyrounakis, George, Mara Nikolaidou, and Michael Hatzopoulos. 2014. "Building Digital Collections Using Open Source Digital Repository Software: A Comparative Study." *International Journal of Digital Library Systems (IJDLS)* 4 (1): 13.

Ritterbush, Jon. 2007. "Supporting Library Research with Libx and Zotero: Two Open Source Firefox Extensions." *Journal of Web Librarianship* 1 (3): 111–22.

St. Laurent, Andrew. 2004. *Understanding Open Source and Free Software Licensing*. Beijing: O'Reilly.

Samuels, Ruth Gallegos, and Henry Griffy. 2012. "Evaluating Open Source Software for Use in Library Initiatives: A Case Study Involving Electronic Publishing." *portal: Libraries and the Academy* 12 (1): 41–62.

Sarma, Gautam Kumar. 2016. "OPAC Module in Open Source Library Management Software: A Comparative Study." *DESIDOC Journal of Library & Information Technology* 36 (1).

Schmidt, Cynthia M., and Teresa L. Hartman. 2015. "Guide on the Side." *Journal of the Medical Library Association* 103 (3): 163.

Shaikh, Maha, and Tony Cornford. 2011. *Total Cost of Ownership of Open Source Software*. A Report for the UK Cabinet Office supported by OpenForum Europe.

Singh, Vandana. 2013. "Why Migrate to an Open Source ILS? Librarians with Adoption Experience Share Their Reasons and Experiences." *Libri* 63 (3): 206–19.

———. 2014a. "Expectations versus Experiences: Librarians Using Open Source Integrated Library Systems." *Electronic Library* 32 (5): 688–709.

———. 2014b. "Open Source Software Use in Libraries: Implications for Social Justice?" *Qualitative & Quantitative Methods in Libraries*.

Steinmacher, Igor, Marco Aurelio Graciotto Silva, Marco Aurelio Gerosa, and David F. Redmiles. 2015. "A Systematic Literature Review on the Barriers Faced by Newcomers to Open Source Software Projects." *Information and Software Technology* 59: 67–85.

Thacker, Curtis, and Charles Knutson. 2015. "Barriers to Initiation of Open Source Software Projects in Libraries." *code4Lib Journal* 29.

Thacker, Curtis J., Charles D. Knutson, and Mark Dehmlow. 2014. *SPEC Kit 340 Open Source Software*. Washington, D.C.: Association of Research Libraries. Accessed May 15, 2016. http://publications.arl.org/Open-Source-Software-SPEC-Kit-340/6.

Wang, Yongming, and Trevor A. Dawes. 2012. "The Next Generation Integrated Library System: A Promise Fulfilled." *Information Technology and Libraries* 31 (3): 76.

Whitfield, Sharon. 2011. "Implementing CORAL: An Electronic Resource Management System." *Computers in Libraries* 31 (8): 19.

Witten, Ian H., Stefan J. Boddie, David Bainbridge, and Rodger J. McNab. 2000. "Greenstone: A Comprehensive Open-Source Digital Library Software System." In *Proceedings of the Fifth ACM Conference on Digital Libraries*. 113–21.

Yamauchi, Yutaka, Makoto Yokozawa, Takeshi Shinohara, and Toru Ishida. 2000. "Collaboration with Lean Media: How Open-Source Software Succeeds." In *Proceedings of the 2000 ACM Conference on Computer Supported Cooperative Work*. 329–38.

Yang, Sharon Q., and Melissa A. Hofmann. 2010. "The Next Generation Library Catalog: A Comparative Study of the OPACs of Koha, Evergreen, and Voyager." *Information Technology and Libraries* 29 (3): 141–50.

Yuvaraj, Mayank, and Ambrish Kumar Maurya. 2016. "Open Source Hardware in Libraries: An Introduction and Overview." *Library Hi Tech News* 33 (4).

Chapter Eight

Early Adoption, Early Abandonment

Parallel Problems in Promoting New Technology

Caitlin A. Bagley

Academic libraries have found themselves increasingly trying to balance the needs of students who lie at both extremes of use; particularly within an information literacy lens, we can deal with students who have already been exposed to higher levels of information literacy, and those who are completely unexposed. Those who will not stray from printed material and those who are willing to try anything once. Both of these users need the help of the library, but trying to find the right approach without scaring off the other can be frustrating. The Foley Library at Gonzaga University has approached this from different angles by adopting a series of differing technologies to varying levels of success. Although there have been many technologies that have been adopted successfully without much hindrance, it is also important to seriously examine why certain adopted technologies fail to flourish when others did so easily. This chapter aims to look at two technologies that the library attempted to adopt and in particular what aided or hindered their total adoption by library staff and by students by looking at the literature of technology adoption and abandonment.

APPROACHES TO ADOPTION

As a masters level, midsize university, the Foley Library at Gonzaga consists of ten faculty librarians and more than twenty-five staff members. The library had the flexibility to try new things without risk of major fallout so long as things were brought out on a small scale so that innovations could be approached slowly. Indeed, there is a spirit of trial and error at the library

95

where new ideas and projects are frequently brought up and tried, but along with this comes the necessary function that not everything makes the final cut toward continued and long-term use. The library serves more than seven thousand FTE (full-time equivalent) undergraduate and graduate students both in person and online. This private liberal arts school has focused on educating the whole person, and with that mission, the library has tended toward collections and technologies that students use and will need for their direct education. Although the IT department is housed primarily within the library building itself, there has been a clear bifurcation of the two units, and this has been reflected in how some technologies have been supported through their adoption at the library. Without total support from both departments, many technologies have been adopted by both sides, but few have succeeded completely across both departments. This chapter will highlight the software technologies Jing and Piktochart to show what worked and did not in their adoption. Both of these resources were brought into the library through similar means, but they were received entirely differently. Jing was seen in a confused light by many staff members, and was ultimately abandoned in no small part because of this confusion, whereas Piktochart was ultimately adopted due in part by staff anticipation of its uses and reception.

LITERATURE REVIEW

As the literature was reviewed about technology adoption and abandonment, one of the most common notions to recur throughout was the "diffusion of innovations theory" (Rogers 2003), which focuses on the life cycle of how an innovation technology is embraced and entered into the life cycle of an institution. Many noted that their particular institutions followed the natural life cycle of adoption: knowledge, persuasion, decision, implementation, and confirmation. Another way of looking at it is that there is the innovation itself, and there are varying communication channels, time, and the social system that the innovation will be applied toward. However, as Heidi Blackburn (2011, 663–77) states, "IT implementation is often the most difficult, not only because of varying technological skills, but because each librarian may not have fully been made aware of the changes." As will be mentioned later, this became a common issue with some of the technology implemented by the Foley Library. It is important to note that although this focuses primarily on technology, the innovation can apply to anything adopted into a culture. Abby Johnson (2016, 58) gives the wise advice to "know why you're making changes, and inform your staff so that they can relay the message to patrons." When a technological service suddenly disappears, patrons can feel left out of the loop. Even if only a few were using the service, those can sometimes be the most vocal. Another important factor that determines the success of any change relies on who implements the change, and what kind of change is being brought about. Fatih Oguz (2016) notes that "technological innovations are generally more observable, have higher triability, and are perceived to be more beneficial, simpler, and easier to implement than administrative innovations." Administrative innovations in relation to technological ones tend to be more focused on organization structure and strategic documentation. Again and again, ease of use was stressed throughout the literature, boiled down to the following statement: "Given that perceived ease-of-use is defined in terms of effort, individuals generally perceive a technology to require less effort to use as they gain more knowledge and confidence through direct experience with the technology" (Kulviwat, Bruner, and Neelankavil 2014, 190–99). The literature seemed to hold that although there was a general pattern in place for all adoption, there were crucial moments where it could go wrong depending how it was supported; in particular, pain points tended to focus on a lack of clarity in directions or assumptions of readiness. Technology that was abandoned tended to be brought in rapidly or without much research on user support for a product.

Critically, many parts of adoption rest on the shoulders of collaboration and multiple skill sets. As Stuart Macdonald and Luis Martinez-Uribe (2010, 5) point out, "These strategies require multidisciplinary skills . . . the alignment of specialists from the aforementioned backgrounds is an important step on the route to a cohesive infrastructure to support researchers." In order to ensure the success of a technology adoption, it is better to have many voices involved including those who will be using the product in any tangible way. In part, this often relies on learning how users interact with a product or what they require from a service point, also known as the user experience (UX). Sometimes this will involve a lot of pretesting with students and others who will use the end product. In the case of Piktochart, there was an initial training session to work out the flaws in how it was taught. During the planning portion it is worthwhile to think broadly about who might be involved with a technology's use. Lauren Kolod and Barbara Unger (2016, 22–27) discuss how their collaborative work started out small, but grew to include others as their work grew. Perhaps obviously only in retrospect, their work thrived because they responded to the feedback they received about changes. Technology changes are often reliant on user-tested improvements and involve many different hands, and are rarely ready out of the box. Roy Schmidt et al. (2001, 9) put it this way: "Today's applications often reach outside the organization and their development involves numerous parties and complicated organizational structures." Leadership literature focuses primarily on receiving feedback about new technology, but in particular, Cara Marco (2015, 46) stresses, "When I discarded secondhand information, I sometimes found myself working with no information at all." Secondhand information in this case refers specifically to what others may have heard about a product or observed indirectly; few have direct knowledge of how a product may actually work. Administration must overcome the challenges of listening to multiple streams of how technology is perceived, used, and desired by their staff without seeming to ignore or disregard the voices of those who might fear approaching administration either because of a sense that administration will not listen to their concerns or because of how much money has already been put toward the product.

PIKTOCHART: EARLY ADOPTION

At the start of the fall semester in 2013, one librarian prepared to teach a series of one-shot instruction courses using infographics as a basis for explaining statistics and census data. At the time, the librarians were working with the ACRL Information Literacy Standards, and were hoping to teach toward Standard Three: "The information literate student evaluates information and its sources critically and incorporates selected information into his or her knowledge base and value system" (Association of College & Research Libraries 2000). There were many software options available at the time for students to generate infographics. And it was hoped that by incorporating a technology like infographic generation, the students would learn ways of filtering and incorporating information from multiple locations. As with many choices to adopt new technologies in the library, this choice came down to price and ease of use. Piktochart, a "freemium" website open to the public, was chosen as the best of many infographic generators by the librarian leading the infographic instruction. Freemium resources differ from free open source software in that they usually only offer a portion of their services for free, with a hook or other options (that give more than the free model) that need to be purchased later. A famous example is Dropbox, which gives free limited storage, but for a paid subscription will give more storage and more data protection. The top reasons Piktochart was chosen were based on the fact that it was a free resource for students that they could all access, the facets and filters were all clearly labeled, and it seemed to be the most approachable of others compared. At the time this included easel.ly and infogr.am, though many more have sprung up in the time since. In later years, the arrival of more generators would create more confusion for students and staff about which generator they were supposed to use. The generator was chosen in part because it was a free resource for the majority of what students would need. Although it had templates that only paid users could access, it had easy-to-start free templates that could be quickly jumped into for those who had never used the software before. Another positive lay in the fact that accounts could be created using e-mail, Facebook accounts, or Google accounts. This was seen as a good advantage, because student e-mail accounts were through Google. These were all things that made it seem as though students would be able to create accounts with minimal hassle. As these would be fifty-minute one-shot sessions, all time needed to be carefully used without a minute wasted, and the librarian wanted to smooth over all potential speed bumps for using the service. Prior to teaching the course, a short trial run had been done with student workers and some staff members. The trial had shown that the concept of infographic instruction worked, but there were some parts of demonstrating Piktochart that required more instruction and advance setup. Attempts were made by the dean of the library at looking into the possibility of purchasing a site license for students, but the only way that could have been done was to create individual accounts devoted to each student. In the end there was no proxy log-in option, and all students were told to create an account prior to arriving to class by the librarian.

One of the downfalls of not paying for a service is that you have no control over not only the services offered, but in terms of knowing when updates will happen, or getting support. When a component of the software breaks, the user can experience a lack of support or feedback on what has gone wrong. At least with paid services, the library usually has a heads-up when new upgrades will be coming and there is a vendor representative that can be contacted in case of trouble. With Piktochart, the library was reliant on contacting customer service or FAQ pages for any help they may have needed. In addition to these pitfalls, Michel Schreiner and Thomas Hess (2013) note, "Instead of charging a fee, other revenue sources can be used, such as monetizing user information by collection storing, analyzing, and even selling it." With such massive privacy concerns, librarians are in a unique position of having to find low-cost opportunities while also safeguarding and making their students knowledgeable about the inherent risks of using a tool. Before each class using Piktochart, the librarian made sure to address the class about the value of understanding where this information would be disseminated, and why it was important to be accurate with their statistics and use of information. In the case of the Foley Library, although there had been several trial runs of the class using staff members and student workers during the summer, there had not been a true class-like scenario until the day of the first class. The prior trial runs had involved gathering those who were available during the summertime and having them create accounts, where they were highly encouraged to play and see what they could do with the service. Student workers who were on hand reported liking it, but their descriptions of any particular problems were often vague, and there was no chance to follow up on what those particular problems were. In short, trials were run quickly with little chance for thoughtful assessment. It was during this initial run that problems already began to arise. Simple problems like the timeline of how the class structure needed to be arranged were shown in clarity, because it quickly became apparent that teaching Piktochart would require a lot of technology explanation before actually using it in class; but larger problems such as the fact that Piktochart does not function well in an Internet Explorer or Safari environment had not been foreseen. In part, this was because most of the staff had used Firefox or Chrome and had not thought to try out other options. While this was a small oversight, it was one that resulted in significant confusion for student users and instructors for some time until it was figured out through trial and error that the cause was browser based. Adopting a freemium technology like this opened the door to these potential problems.

As stated above, one librarian had spearheaded the adoption of this technology, and with this led to siloing of information. When questions about use came into reference, despite alerts about impending questions, there were still staff who were unaware of the product or were unsure of whom to direct the question to. This was not necessarily the fault of the librarian who spearheaded its adoption; it was simply that with no administrative-level support of a technology that would not be used by everyone, there was bound to be some confusion over just who was using which product. To have one person know the most about a product can make the technology really well supported from one side, but it also has the downfall of making the product either inaccessible or at minimum creating unneeded barriers that may prevent the user from actually using the service. Lack of communication creates the problem; as with many communication issues, the more widely it is discussed by the library as a whole, the less problems there will be down the line. With time, more librarians began to use the service, and in one notable case, a faculty member outside the library even began to use it regularly in her classes. This was a clear case of the product becoming more familiar to staff as they experienced it, but it most certainly was not a case of immediate adoption and embrace. Indeed, this adoption has flourished with time as more and more classes are exposed to it each year, and more instruction librarians become familiar with it and use it in their classes. The initial trial went well, but the adoption of Piktochart would have gone better with more trial testing, especially focused among the instruction librarians. As was experienced by the case of California State University, San Marcos, they noted quickly that "using low cost or free software may help alleviate some of the expenditures, but the production/delivery may still be a stress factor for some librarians" (Olivas and Chan 2013, 40–52). Learning any new technology can cause stress in an environment, and it's important not to get caught into the trap of thinking that because the software is a free resource it will have an easier rollout than any other paid product.

Some things that could have been done to alleviate pain points would have been to make the library staff more aware of the LibGuide, perhaps even linking to Piktochart directly from the databases page, despite the fact that it is not a classic database. This linking did not initially happen because it was a pilot project, but later it was likely more of an oversight than any specific lack of trust in the product. At the time of initial implementation, LibGuides had not reached peak use at the library, and there had not been a clear directive on how they would be used from the library. One considera-tion that comes into play when promoting the work of another company such as Piktochart is that the librarian is essentially performing unpaid advertising and marketing work for a company that usually has no intent to reimburse. Piktochart is a very user-friendly site that actively solicits and replies to user feedback, and while this can be a boon to a librarian looking to offer a dynamic service to students who will be responsive, it is also worth looking into the hidden costs of a product that a company promotes. Another option for promotion would be to have a library-wide demonstration of the product before it is used in a classroom setting, along with perhaps a hands-on dem-onstration, a virtual sandbox of sorts. This would have allowed staff to understand potential questions that might have arisen. A small version of this was done, but the focus of the demonstration was not on potential questions, but rather on teaching technique and timing for the course to make sure that the actual class would run smoothly. In retrospect, this time would likely have been better spent if at least a small portion of the time was allotted for addressing potential questions about access that may have arisen at reference. However, the author does acknowledge that sometimes it is hard to get total staff involvement on a product that will not directly affect them in the day to day. Other possibilities would be to alert people on reference that a class is about to be taught and there may be a heightened amount of questions about Piktochart in the coming hours or days. This allows for reference staff to quickly brush up on the tool at the time of need rather than bracing for an unknown and unspecified time when a question might be asked. To refer back to the diffusion of innovations theory, there are often different rates of adoption based upon "perceived attributes of innovations" that include: rela-tive advantage, compatibility, complexity, trialability, and observability. Two of these aspects are highlighted with the adoption of Piktochart, espe-cially observability, which holds that when an innovation's results are easy for others to see, it will be adopted more quickly. The same for complexity, which relates to how an innovation is perceived to be difficult or easy to use. Piktochart was initially perceived by those in the library as being difficult to use, but with more exposure and observation, users began to see that the resource was something that could aid them.

Although planning and logistics problems arise as you add more people to the mix, things tend to go smoother when there is more staff to buy into a product, or as Sarah Houghton-Jan (2007) writes, "Have the sense to realize when decisions are best left to management and when they are best made by the task force." The lack of staff buy-in came both from a sense that this was an instruction tool, and not something other librarians would need to use, and likewise, the lesson plan it was used with was paired closely with statistical datasets, and there may have been an intimidation factor before librarians began to see that Piktochart could be used in other ways. In some senses, easier said than done, but usually if a committee or an administration is sensing opposition, they should start listening to the staff to get a greater sense of why. Others like Julie Evener have focused on ways of garnering buy-in by looking at structured methods: "The best way to propose an idea to decision makers is to know your audience, plan your presentation, and make it as easy as possible for stakeholders to say yes by demonstrating the idea's importance to institutional goals and mission" (Evener 2015, 296–311). This relies on institutions and librarians to be aware of these goals and missions. If there is any sense of uncertainty or lack of clarity about these things, then it becomes harder to drive people around central ideas and needs. All in all, Piktochart has been a successful rollout in that it is still actively used across campus by many instructors and librarians. There are certainly those who use it more than others, but this would be the case in any technological rollout. It was not smooth, but it has migrated successfully into a used application.

JING: EARLY ABANDONMENT

For those who have not yet used it, Jing is screen-capturing software published by TechSmith that has been widely used by libraries and others to upload quick tutorial videos to the web. The software was first created in 2007 but did not gain wide use in libraries for a few years as it faced a slow rollout. A perfect example of this unfamiliarity was that when discussing when Jing was adopted, staff members of Foley could not come to a clear consensus of when exactly the service had been implemented at the library. The rollout was so slow and done through only a few computers at a time, that many people were initially unaware of the product. Comments ranged from "I don't know when it was added, because I never used it" to "It had to be within the last three years, because I know it was since I was in this position." Keeping such viewpoints in mind, it was eventually narrowed down that Jing was most likely installed on the reference computer during the summer of 2013. Through this winnowing, it was discovered that only one staff member was using the product with regularity, and the videos created tended to be for explanations to vendors and the IT department. While it was a relief to discover that the product was being used by someone, such comments reveal the problems with adding in a new technology. The Foley Library is a relatively small library of about thirty staff members that is supported by the university IT support system. There is a library staff member who acts as the IT manager and liaison who helps the university IT understand the unique needs of library technology. However, without institution-wide support or, at the minimum, support from library administration or supervisors, staff can feel there is no reason to learn the tool or even to keep up to date on it. Staff at the Foley Library also varied in how willing and capable they were to adapt to new technologies. While some were willing to learn new technology, many felt that they did not have the time to learn something new unless it was absolutely essential to their job. Few took it upon themselves to investigate what a new tool might be on their own unless they were motivated by an outside influence.

Added with the idea of making short videos to send over chat or e-mail to distance education students (among others) to demonstrate how to navigate varying websites and databases, in practice, it became more clutter and nuisance than actual practical tool. The reasons for this focused on misunderstanding of who should use it, no overall training, and no support. There are several comparisons that can be made to the Piktochart adoption in that once again this was a technological adoption that was largely spearheaded by one person as opposed to being brought on by a group or administration. The primary differences, though, seem to lie in the fact that there was no distinct user group or class attached to the idea. Piktochart eventually flourished after other teachers and instructors were exposed to the idea, but with the case of Jing, there was no attempt at evangelization and the product was essentially left to be used by only one person. Although technologies can be adopted organically as people notice what works and does not work, it generally takes a strong leader or voice to convince others that a particular technology should be adopted not just by one but by the entire institution. One concern brought up by Praveen Aggarwal, Taihoon Cha, and David Wilemon (1998, 358–71) was, "Limited data on actual product performance and limited experience with the product or product category are likely to cause consumers to experience greater uncertainty and risk." When the majority of library staff were unfamiliar with the product, they had little making them desire to learn it and stray from what they already knew how to use.

Jing quickly became clutter on the reference desktop that was more likely to be accidentally clicked on than intentionally so. Indeed, the one staff member who worked with Jing most frequently said, "The annoying thing about Jing is the 'sun' tool. It's nice because it's always easy to use it to grab a screenshot, but it seems to get in the way no matter where you move it" (Spracklen 2016). Indeed, it was because of that very sun tool, which allows a user to quickly make a video without having to find and select the application, that most people were aware of it at all. It is very easy to accidentally click on and start up a video without intending to. For a while, many people were confused about why a sun was appearing on the screen when they went to print or answer a chat. In practice, when the application opened up, it was usually quickly closed out by someone who was not actually looking for it.

This was a design flaw that was well intentioned but did not take into account that there would be multiple users on the same computer. One strategy that might have helped to make Jing work better would have been to place Jing only on select computers that would be used only by one user. Although reference seems like a natural spot to place Jing, by its very nature, the reference desk deals with a constant change of hands as librarians take shifts working there. This leads to natural information loss, because each user treats individual machines and software slightly differently.

Aside from the fact that no one was fully aware of the power of Jing, another major reason for its failure to thrive was that the distance services librarian and others who were more likely to use a screen-capturing software had already paid for Camtasia Studios (also by TechSmith), and were heavily invested in it. There was concern that if tutorials were offered through both Camtasia and through Jing that there would be an inconsistent message that might be confusing for some students. The two tools were designed for very different versions of screensharing, with Jing intended to be quick and granular level, and Camtasia focused on longer overviews. Perhaps some of the initial frustration came from trying to use Jing in place of Camtasia, when the product is not necessarily made for that style of production. Still, if the users who are the most natural choices for adoption are not willing or do not see the reason for adoption, it will be a major uphill battle to make the product thrive. Jing has many merits, but one of its primary competitors is a product offered by its own parent company. These competing desires most likely have an effect on how products are marketed and which fields they are brought into. In the screensharing world, Camtasia is a well-known powerhouse, and perhaps some of the failure to thrive by Jing was dealt by the fact that Camtasia was already so well established in the field. Likewise, Jing was adopted because one staff member was more familiar with it than with Camtasia and wanted to try it. One of the benefits of a small-staffed library is that it gives people the ability to adopt technology with such ease and little resistance, especially as there was an attitude that perhaps Camtasia was not the only option and it was worth exploring a new option, especially if it was free. Notably, Jing used to have a paid option called Jing Pro that was introduced in 2009, but by 2013 TechSmith had fully retired the Pro version. TechSmith has many screensharing software platforms besides Jing and Camtasia, and with the Pro version now retired, it would be wise to monitor support for the product.

One of the biggest problems with any technology product brought into the library is that support may eventually disappear or die out with libraries having to maintain legacy software that may no longer be compatible with the technology of the future. Libraries, especially state and public libraries, are increasingly dealing with shrinking or stagnant budgets that are being asked to stretch further than before. With these concerns in mind, it's only natural that a library director would be looking for a free resource that could cover perceived future needs. Free things often have hidden and unforeseen costs, though, including the loss of staff time as they take time to learn a new technology. Any new technology would require staff to take time to learn it, but when considering total costs it's important to consider how much training would be expected. It is not always clear with free resources. In 2012, even the *Information World Review* noted that ROI is frequently touted as the best way to get the financial picture of using a new technology, but there are other factors to consider including total cost of ownership (TCO). These items can get lost in the appeal of a new technology. Still they emphasize, "It is far easier and less costly to change a decision when it is still on the drawing board" ("Migrating to the Cloud" 2012). The cost of frequent changes goes beyond just the cost of investing in the purchase price of a technology—it also can affect staff attitudes as things change too rapidly, making them lose confidence in administration or the technology. Some costs hidden in the TCO that people might not consider when choosing software are things Dale Hockel and Michael Kintner (2014, 16–17) mention, like "utilities, upgrades, CE costs, training and disposal." One might ask, if all prior versions of a technology have failed to last long in an environment, why should a staff member invest labor in learning a new method that if it follows trend, will likely disappear shortly? However, one of the key points of the diffusion of innovations theory focuses on the types of adopters that bring new technologies into their lives: early adopters, early majority, late majority, and laggards. Each role has its own decision-making process and reasoning for bringing a technology into use. Perhaps the library staff members who had to deal with Jing had differing adoption styles, with the staff member who brought in Jing using it being more used to an early majority style, with others being more part of the late majority or even laggard style. At the Foley Library there is not currently a standardized technology adoption plan, and often things are adopted at the point of need sometimes by the staff at large, and sometimes things slowly filter into use from early adopters who can lead others into the new technology with skill. Ultimately, Jing did not have a planning portion for how it was implemented at the Foley Library. Without such planning, there was no structure in place to help Jing find a home within the library. Lori Reed (2010) summarizes the problems with training staff on new technology as follows: "Self-paced training often appeals to self-directed learners who are highly motivated." While the field does tend to draw self-directed learners, there is always a struggle in trying to motivate those who lack it for whatever reason.

CONCLUSION

There will always be new innovations and technologies to be adopted within the library world, but as experience and the literature review has shown, if there is not strong support for the innovation itself, there will be a struggle. Although it is not necessarily doomed to failure, the adoption rate can be hindered and significantly slowed by misunderstandings and lack of support. Likewise, if a technology is not perceived as easy to use, it can fail to thrive when users are intimidated by the product, as in the case of Jing. Strong leadership from administration or vocal staff members is not an absolute, but it can help determine attitude when training begins. Without a well-thought-out implementation, the adoption will succeed or fail based solely on its merits, which will be up to individuals to determine on their own without input.

Most technology adoptions can and will go well, but it should be noted that as accelerating technological change comes to libraries, better plans for adoption should be developed sooner so that future adoptions and implementations can go smoothly. If not, technology failure will be a frequent scenario until the library unilaterally decides to adopt. The diffusion of innovations theory has been around for decades now, and while it is not required that a library follow the methods detailed within it for success, and indeed, it should not be seen as a prescriptive method for success, merely an observation of how many innovations roll out, libraries should likely consider familiarizing themselves with the methods in order to help smooth over a better transition. As many libraries are focusing on new ways to bring about change in their libraries, it would serve them well to look toward the business models and theories of other fields to see how they could potentially apply in the library. Technologies in and of themselves will not make or break an adoption; it is the people who bring the technologies into use.

REFERENCES

Aggarwal, Praveen, Taihoon Cha, and David Wilemon. 1998. "Barriers to the Adoption of Really-New Products and the Role of Surrogate Buyers." *Journal of Consumer Marketing* 15 (4): 358–71.

Association of College & Research Libraries. 2000. *Information Literacy Competency Standards for Higher Education.*

Blackburn, Heidi. 2011. "Millennials and the Adoption of New Technologies in Libraries through the Diffusion of Innovations Process." *Library Hi Tech* 29 (4): 663–77.

Evener, Julie. 2015. "Innovation in the Library: How to Engage Employees, Cultivate Creativity, and Create Buy-In for New Ideas." *College & Undergraduate Libraries* 22 (3): 296–311.

Hockel, Dale, and Michael Kintner. 2014. "Uncovering the Real Total Cost of Ownership: The Influence of Clinical Engineering." *Health Management Technology* 35 (10): 16–17.

Houghton-Jan, Sarah. 2007. "Staff Participation and Buy-In." *Library Technology Reports* 43 (2): 26–28.

Johnson, Abby. 2016. "Pulling the Plug." *American Libraries* 47 (5): 58.

Kolod, Lauren, and Barbara Unger. 2016. "A Collaborative Journey: The Learning Commons." *Teacher Librarian* 43 (4): 22–27.

Kulviwat, Songpol, Gordon C. Bruner II, and James P. Neelankavil. 2014. "Self-Efficacy as an Antecedent of Cognition and Affect in Technology Acceptance." *Journal of Consumer Marketing* 31 (3): 190–99.

Macdonald, Stuart, and Luis Martinez-Uribe. 2010. "Collaboration to Data Curation: Harnessing Institutional Expertise." *New Review of Academic Librarianship* 16: 4–16.

Marco, Cara. 2015. "Lessons from a Leader's First Year." *Library Journal* 140 (14): 46.

"Migrating to the Cloud Has Hidden Costs." 2012. *Information World Review*, 3–5.

Oguz, Fatih. 2016. "Organizational Influences in Technology Adoption Decisions: A Case Study of Digital Libraries." *College & Research Libraries* 77 (3): 314–34.

Olivas, Antonia P., and Ian Chan. 2013. "Beyond the Reference Desk: A Study on the Effectiveness of Low-Cost Distance Library Services at California State University San Marcos." *Journal of Library & Information Services in Distance Learning* 7 (1): 40–52.

Reed, Lori. 2010. "When the Going Gets Tough, the Staff Needs More Training." *Computers in Libraries* 30 (3): 6–11.

Rogers, Everett M. 2003. *Diffusion of Innovations*. 5th ed. New York: Free Press.

Schmidt, Roy, Kalle Lyytinen, Mark Keil, and Paul Cule. 2001. "Identifying Software Project Risks: An International Delphi Study." *Journal of Management Information Systems* 17 (4): 5–36.

Schreiner, Michel, and Thomas Hess. 2013. "On the Willingness to Pay for Privacy as a Freemium Model: First Empirical Evidence." *ECIS 2013 Research in Progress Paper 30*.

Spracklen, John (interlibrary loan supervisor). 2016. Interview by Caitlin A. Bagley, May 20. Interview transcript.

Chapter Nine

A Model to Align Technology with Strategy and Structure in Academic Libraries

Harish Maringanti

While there may not be complete agreement in the specifics regarding the future of academic libraries, there seems to be a broad consensus on the need for them to rethink how they invest their resources (human, facilities, technology, etc.) to create relevant programs that align with ever-evolving teaching and research missions (Jaggars 2014). Library thought leaders have proposed various pathways such as implementing business process reengineering methods for finding operational efficiencies, reskilling existing staff, or recruiting staff with different professional preparation to support new service models (Auckland 2012) to move us forward in these times of increased scrutiny and financial pressures. Leveraging technology is central to most of those ideas, but there has been very little discussion to date on the importance of alignment between technology, strategy, and structure. This is what will be explored in this chapter—deploying the best piece of technology doesn't make an organization great. In the hunt for the "best product" they sometimes lose sight of what it takes to successfully appropriate technologies—deploying it alone is not an end in itself.

This chapter seeks to describe broader issues related to technology and its relationship to the strategy and structure in academic libraries and offers one perspective in addressing these issues to the current and emerging library leaders. The rest of this chapter is organized into four sections. Section 1 sets the context for this chapter by diving into the changing landscape of higher education and the role of academic libraries. Section 2 focuses on the impact of technology in organizations. Section 3 will look at the impact of the integrated library system on academic libraries and discuss the relationship between technology, strategy, and structure. Section 4 will include a brief discussion of the literature in business, information studies (IS), and other disciplines as it relates to technology, strategy, and structure. A simple framework proposed by Gartner will be introduced in this section to describe demands on any IT organization along with corresponding expectations. A discussion on how this framework would translate to general IT operations in academic libraries and how to integrate organizational strategy with the organizational structure will follow. I make no claims as to the completeness of my perspective, and present here my opinions (as a technologist) in the hopes of adding to the current stream of thinking about technology in academic libraries.

SECTION 1: CHANGING LANDSCAPE OF HIGHER EDUCATION AND ROLE OF ACADEMIC LIBRARIES

Rather than focus on the library as an independent entity and discuss its changing nature, Denise Troll (2002) puts this in a broader context and says, "Whether the fundamental mission of libraries has changed may be a matter of interpretation or local policy, but the environment and circumstances in which libraries pursue their mission is dramatically different from the environment and circumstances of the past." The environment today is indeed very different with a different set of challenges than in the past. Today's challenging environment includes, as Clifford Lynch (2000) puts it, the "publishing and information marketplace, changing modalities of scholarly communication, and evolving capabilities in the user community." With technologies such as virtual reality, augmented reality, machine learning, and advanced digital fabrication moving into the mainstream, the boundaries of users' capabilities are expanding and their expectations are only getting bigger day by day. The shift seen in "students as consumers to students as creators," as outlined in the New Media Consortium's *Horizon Report* (New Media Consortium 2014), is one such result that affects the higher education community significantly and has implications for technology offerings within academic libraries.

The operating models of higher education, the immediate context within which academic libraries operate (organizationally), have seen many changes in the recent past and will undoubtedly face more scrutiny with the cost of higher education becoming a political hot topic. Falling revenues from enrollment, government, and other sources; rising demands for a greater return on investment in higher education; greater transparency about student outcomes; emerging business and delivery models; and globalization of education—these forces are reshaping higher education as per a report published by Boston Consulting Group in 2014 (Henry et al. 2014).

Libraries have responded to these challenges in a myriad of ways—by spawning makerspaces within the existing physical facilities, by coming up with new assessment metrics, by shifting their strategy from a collection-centric approach to an engagement-centric approach. While some of these forces have been at play for some time, the increasing competition for the same dollar and libraries' inability to articulate their value has contributed to reshaping the environment in a more challenging way to navigate for the libraries (Gibson and Dixon 2011).

In a report dating back to 1968, Robert F. Munn describes libraries as bottomless pits in his article (Munn 1968). That report, though fifty years old, is still relevant today and the perception issues persist, as is evident in the conclusion of a study done at Indiana University of Pennsylvania (IUP) in 2010 in which the authors noted, "Because there is so much information available to faculty and students through the internet, college and university administrators are beginning to question the role of academic libraries" (Heider et al. 2012, 18). More recent research findings from Ithaka S+R clearly identify a perception gap between the perceptions of faculty and administration regarding the library's role versus library directors' perceptions of their roles (Long and Schonfeld 2014, 36). For example, faculty members were much less likely to agree with the statement "Librarians help students to develop their research skills" than were library directors. Though going in depth into the challenges facing libraries is not the purpose of this chapter, laying out the environment that the libraries find themselves in today sets the stage for the rest of this chapter. Suffice it to say that academic libraries find themselves in a rapidly changing environment and in these times of need, academic library leaders can create a stable foundation to build new programs and initiatives by making thoughtful investments in technology and aligning technology strategy with their business goals.

SECTION 2: IT IMPACTS ORGANIZATIONAL OUTPUTS

Worldwide, higher education sector spending on IT is forecast to grow 1.2 percent to reach (U.S.) $38.2 billion in 2016, according to Gartner (2016). Agencies are making these investments in IT because they recognize the value add that IT brings to the education sector. While discussing economic growth and technological progress, Joel Mokyr, a famous economic historian, writes, "Technological progress has been one of the most potent forces in history in that it has provided society with what economists call 'free lunch,' i.e., an increase in output that is not commensurate with the increase in effort and cost necessary to bring it about" (Mokyr 1992). This statement captures the very essence of investing in technology for productivity gains. Citing Thomas Whisler's research, Ali Farhanghi, Abbas Abbaspour, and

Reza Ghassemi (2013) write, "Whisler hypothesized that IT would have a tremendous influence upon the structure of the organization, resulting in fewer employees, a narrower span of control, a reduction in the organizational levels. The influence of IT would not be limited to a single department but would have a dramatic impact throughout the organization."

There are two broad issues that technologists working in higher education need to be cognizant about:

1. IT productivity paradox: A tendency for computerization to fail to improve standard measures of productivity (Bowen 2012). While discussing productivity in higher education, William Bowen notes that IT had a big impact on higher education in the last few decades but it has been primarily in "output-enhancing" ways. To put it simply, as some researchers looking into this issue have noted, the "important dimensions of service output such as accessibility and convenience—factors that are greatly improved by IT—are difficult to quantify and are rarely captured by productivity metrics" (Jones et al. 2012). For example, in academic libraries, services such as seamless delivery of electronic resources (via interlibrary loan), discovery tools, and so forth, save the time of the user, but this is not captured by traditional measures of productivity. Until assessment techniques can incorporate qualitative measurements and measure academic libraries' contributions toward educational outcomes, it will always be challenging to measure IT's role in the success of an academic library's mission. If productivity is simply defined as ratio of outputs to inputs, then it is hard to measure IT's contributions as there exists no current standards to meaningfully measure convenience or user experience. Bowen (2012) argues that "we need to improve productivity through determined efforts to reduce costs—that we need to focus more energy on lowering the denominator of the productivity ratio" (which is the inputs). Simply put, this means doing more with less.

2. Cost disease: Bowen coined the term "cost disease" to mean the phenomenon that is prevalent in labor-intensive industries such as the performing arts and education, where there is less opportunity than in other sectors to increase productivity by, for example, substituting capital for labor. This results in unit labor costs rising relatively faster in these industries than in the economy overall (Bowen 2012).

Given the two broad issues cited above, technology-centric productivity gains is not an easy argument to make. Identifying and deploying a better technology doesn't automatically generate savings in staff time if proper attention is not paid to local organizational context. There is sufficient evidence in the literature that demonstrates that application of identical technologies, in very similar organizational contexts, can often result in radically different organizational impacts (Orlikowski 1992). Overcoming these two issues would require proper alignment between IT strategy, business strategy, and organizational structure (Doherty, Champion, and Wang 2010).

SECTION 3: IMPACT OF ILS ON LIBRARY OPERATIONS

For the better part of history, the focus of technology in libraries has been on the ILS (integrated library system). Peter Brophy and Peter Wynne (1997) proposed a scheme to describe library functions in five broad areas—resource discovery, resource delivery, resource utilization, infrastructure provision, and resource management. Under their proposed scheme, a modern ILS coupled with a discovery tool could fulfill most of the library functions. For example, the latest systems from Ex Libris (Alma/Primo combination) would address four of these five core functions, namely, discovery, delivery, utilization, and management of resources. Needless to say, the ILS has occupied such prominence in the library technology world because it functions as the primary business system to manage internal operations while delivering value to the users. Since the traditional role of academic libraries has been to organize, catalog, and store information (primarily print materials such as books), technology in libraries mainly revolved around the management of print materials. New technological investments in emerging services such as institutional repository (IR), scholarly communication, and digital scholarship only began to happen in the last few decades. Because a single system, such as an ILS, dominated the library operations for so long, it might be prudent to look at the history and lessons learned from implementing the ILS as a technology and the impact it had on organizational structure and strategy. Because of their evolving role, libraries will soon be expected to offer enterprise-wide systems that go beyond an ILS—systems such as digital library systems, research data management systems, and so forth. It is important to discuss the impact on organizational structure and strategy when ILSs were implemented in libraries as lessons learned from this endeavor can frame the strategy for designing technology-rich services in the libraries.

Richard West and Peter Lyman have suggested a three-phase procession of the effects of information technology on organizations: (1) modernization (doing what you are already doing, though more efficiently); (2) innovation (experimenting with new capabilities that the technology makes possible); and (3) transformation (fundamentally altering the nature of the organization through these capabilities) (Lynch 2000). Clifford Lynch used this framework to describe what happened to academic libraries in the latter part of the twentieth century. Laura Kinner and Christine Rigda (2009) expanded on this work in describing the evolution of the automated library system (ALS) into the integrated library system. Modernization, the first phase, occurred during the 1970s and 1980s when systems were "purpose built, stand-alone systems that solved a single problem." Innovation, the second phase, occurred in the late 1980s to early 1990s with the advent of the online public access catalog (OPAC) and the integration of the OPAC with the core library modules. Transformation, the final phase of the procession of the information technol-

ogy, occurred at the beginning of the twenty-first century and involved leveraging networks to tailor services to each user.

Marshall Breeding, while comparing traditional ILSs to the next-generation ILSs, argued that the migration to new ILSs would eliminate many
hardware and maintenance investments for libraries as the new systems are
likely to be hosted in the cloud (software as a service [SaaS] model) (Breeding 2013). This could have a major impact on IT and technical services
staffing levels if many of the functions carried out by local staff can be done
centrally by the vendor. Ping Fu and Moira Fitzgerald (2013) explored this
question in depth (the impact on staffing models when traditional ILSs were
migrated to the next-generation ILSs) and concluded that systems staff might
be able to reduce their workload by approximately 40 percent. A significant
point to remember in this analysis is that the authors compared traditional
ILSs to the new, cloud-based and vendor-provided ILSs only. (Note: This
analysis doesn't take into account the discovery products—invariably all the
new ILSs make use of a discovery tool that acts as the front gateway for users
to interact with the content. But the main point about savings in staff time
still remains even though the percentages may vary.) Breeding speculated
that libraries might have adapted their workflows to limitations in the ILS
(Breeding 2007). Given that the ILS market is dominated by proprietary
systems that may have very little scope for local customizations, any local
workflows need to be accommodated outside of the system. For example, if
local campus systems can export patron data in XML but the vendor ILS
cannot import XML files directly into the system, then custom scripts need to
be developed to crosswalk XML into a format that the vendor system can
understand.

Libraries are not immune to effects of organizational structure on workflows, that is, depending on how resources are organized in the organization,
it is very likely to have an impact on workflows (Iochpe and Thom 2001). It
is much more convenient to change workflows than to change systems. Using the patron data example from above, one could argue that it is easier to
change the patron data loading process than to replace the ILS. This points to
the fact that implementing new technology systems will have an impact on
workflows and staffing. This can lead to structural changes in the organization if a conscious decision is made to redeploy the savings (staff time) into
other emerging initiatives.

The advantage of having a single dominant system in one industry (such
as the library segment of the market) is that we can look toward lessons
learned from other industries where a single product dominated their business operations—a case in point is ERP (enterprise resource planning) systems in manufacturing industries. As the ERP is to manufacturing industries,
so is the ILS to libraries. While digital repositories are a big presence in the
current library operations, their functionality and workflows are still evolv-

ing and do not occupy the same central space that ILSs do in all the libraries. Because of their broad-ranging impact on organizations, research scholars have used the study of ERP implementations and their effect on organizations as a proxy to understand the impacts of IT on organizations. Doherty et al. state, "Not only does ERP present a single and well defined type of software application, which is increasingly common, also the potential of ERP to engender significant organizational impacts has been widely recognized" and "the introduction of a highly integrated ERP system, within a manufacturing company, is likely to have a significant impact on that organization's business processes, structure, culture and enterprise level performance, as well as the motivation, job specifications and performance of individual employees." Their study found that the "implementation of ERP technology and the strategic orientation of the host organization are likely to modify the structural design of organizations and that ERP is more likely to affect structural changes, when deployed in the presence of a complementary 'Prospector' corporate strategy" (Doherty, Champion, and Wang 2010). The core business process management system, be it ERP in manufacturing or ILS in libraries, has an organization-wide impact. ILS and ERP are big enough that their impact is organization-wide and not just limited to one or two departments.

The impact of an ILS on the organization's structure, workflows, and strategy can best be demonstrated by an example. Consider two different scenarios for implementing ILSs—one is a vendor system running in the cloud where all core IT operations are managed by the vendor (backups, security, storage) and the other is an open source system deployed and managed by the local IT department. It is very likely that the organizational chart (structure) in these two scenarios would look completely different—IT resources in the former case might be supporting digital projects while providing minimal support for ILS, whereas, in the latter case, IT would have a much deeper involvement with running ILS operations. One assumption to make at the outset is that every organization (in this case, academic libraries) has a limited set of IT resources. It is up to the leadership to decide where to invest those resources—if the leadership is interested in pursuing the "prospector strategy" that is, branching out into new services (such as 3D printing, data repositories), then choosing a vendor-hosted ILS option might be their logical choice. Business strategy would dictate the selection of the system to implement and that would have an impact on the organizational structure. This discussion about ILS in libraries and ERP in manufacturing companies demonstrates the impact IT has on organizational structure, workflows, and strategy.

SECTION 4: TECHNOLOGY, STRATEGY AND STRUCTURE

Jeremy Rose and Matthew Jones (2005, 19) ask a very interesting question that reflects on the relationship between IT and organizations: "Does IT shape organizations, or do people in organizations control how IT is used?" To formulate the question a little differently: Does agency (the capacity to make a difference) lie predominantly with machines (computer systems) or humans (organizational actors)? Wanda Orlikowski (1992) has discussed this topic at length in various research studies and says: "Early research studies assumed technology to be an objective, external force that would have deterministic impacts on organizational properties such as structure. Later researchers focused on human aspects of technology, seeing it as the outcome of strategic choice and social action."

Citing several research studies in the field of information studies (IS), Doherty, Champion, and Wang (2010) write that there is a growing debate as to whether strategy shapes structure or whether strategy follows structure. The scholars have found that in the long term, strategy both shapes and follows organizational structure, but that the shaping effects of strategy are stronger. François Bergeron, Louis Raymond, and Suzanne Rivard, while discussing strategic alignment and business performance, write that "assuming there is no single best way to invest in IT, theoretical IS (information studies) contingency frameworks have been proposed, purporting to describe and explain the impact of alignment upon performance. Fundamental proposition is that organizational performance is the consequence of fit between two or more factors such as strategy, structure, technology, culture, and environment." Strategy is the force that mediates between the firm and its environment. For an excellent example of how strategy might influence structure, consider an example that is very common in multinational corporations: "It was found that an increasing level of product diversity leads multinational corporations to choose a product division rather than a functional division structure" (Bergeron, Raymond, and Rivard 2004).

Dale Askey and Lisa Janicke Hinchliffe recently wrote: "Given the number and variety of significant information technology (IT) projects supported and led by research libraries, one could incorrectly assume that IT has been successfully integrated into our organizations" (2016). That statement succinctly captures the underlying issue with technology discussions in academic libraries. For far too long, IT has been viewed as a "black box" when library functions are discussed and sometimes adjectives like "cloud" (as in confusing) have been used to describe technology operations. Business leaders often equate IT with utilities (common analogy is its comparison to water and electricity) where, yes, users do not have to know about the ins and outs of IT operations as long as its impact on the business value is clear—for example, whether one deploys Solaris clusters or Linux containers in the local data center or the cloud; or deploys Macs or PCs in the classroom—it should not matter as long as the services are being delivered consistently. The library and its IT department, if it has one, operate within the context of a university with a central campus IT unit. The relationship between library IT and campus IT can be somewhat tenuous owing to the overlap in operations. This creates confusion within library leadership ranks as to what should be handled by campus IT. But there ends the weak argument in favor of using that label to broad-stroke every technology activity in the library as IT. The root cause, as I see it, is with the terminology or lack thereof. This is not an issue confined to just the library domain. Delving into this issue, the prominent organizational theorist Wanda Orlikowski has said, "Despite years of investigative effort there is little agreement on the definition and measurement of technology" (1992). In fact, two broad views have pervaded in the studies of technology regarding its definition: one focused on technology as "hardware"—that is, the machines, equipment that humans use in productive activities; and another focused on "social technologies"—that is, the generic tasks, techniques, and knowledge utilized when humans engage in productive activities (Orlikowski 1992). These views have led to the proliferation of the usage of the term "technology."

IT is a big enterprise with its own subcultures—how systems administrators think and act is much different than how programmers work (the DevOps movement rose to prominence to bridge this gap in cultures); how desktop software is deployed and delivered is much different than data center operations; while scalability is the driving force behind data center operations, it is the speed and scope that might be driving the user interface enhancements (i.e., each IT function tries to optimize a different performance indicator such as speed or scalability, and this leads to the differences in cultures and behaviors of IT specialists). Each aspect of IT comes with its own flavor of organizational constructs—structure, strategy, and culture. Given the different variants, it is always challenging to answer the question "What is the best way to organize IT?" There is no perfect organizational structure that would work for every organization at every time. This search for the right organizational structure may be based on the false belief that there exists a prescriptive, best-practice model that all organizations could employ. Unfortunately, if it were true, there wouldn't have been so much written about it already. It is not the purpose of this chapter nor my intention to describe or prescribe specific organizational structures. Rather, I propose a simple and generic framework to view technology-related activities in the library and will discuss strategies to better align IT with the business goals.

Very broadly put, every organization faces three interrelated, yet distinct, demands for technology services. According to a Gartner research report (Gartner 2016, 4), the principal demands on the IT organization are for IT to: "(i) provide the common technological infrastructure and basic operations needed in the entire enterprise; (ii) evolve and improve the support for business processes and platforms that form the core of the current and immediate future enterprise activities; and (iii) support or lead transformational initiatives that shape the longer-term future products, services and operations of the enterprise." The report goes on to state that each of these demands has different characteristics in terms of delivery focus, relationship with the rest of the enterprise, team/group value proposition, and dominant key performance indicators (KPIs). The report further states that the typical structure for IT organizations are therefore likely to include three main elements: "(i) an infrastructure and operations group, typically transactional in nature and organized along technical skills; (ii) a group focused on the support of core processes. This group tends to collaborate with business units on evolving the process, and is organized around business processes or clusters; and (iii) a transformational group that works closely with business units (BUs) and digital leaders to transform the business unit. This group is typically closely aligned to the BU's structure and may also in terms of objectives and primary KPIs be closer aligned with the BUs than with the rest of IT."

Using this model as a template, it is easy to envision how the IT operations could be structured within academic libraries:

1. Infrastructure and operations group: this is the group that can handle commodity services such as endpoint devices provisioning (desktops, laptops, mobile devices), handling network services (upgrading switches, routers, VOIP services), providing help desk services, handling data center operations (servers, storage), other related activities. Some of these operations are also much more likely to be offered by a central campus IT unit. Libraries can benefit from reflecting upon the unique value proposition that each group offers and eliminate duplicating services where feasible (provided funding and service-level agreements [SLAs] are not an issue).
2. Core business process support group: in library parlance, this group would be primarily charged with supporting the integrated library systems, discovery tools, and so forth.
3. Transformative group: this is where libraries would do well to leverage technology. Entrusting technology leaders to lead emerging initiatives might be a risk worth taking as diverse ideas and solutions are only going to move the profession forward.

With emerging technologies such as virtual desktop infrastructure (VDI), 3D printing, location-aware services, and new ways of getting work done (agile, other project management methodologies), the IT landscape itself is shifting along with users' expectations and one can argue that the line between different segmented functions might be blurring (for example, with the new DevOps model there is no real separation between operations and development groups anymore). IT's functions can be segmented in any number of ways and while the exact number of functional segments isn't a prescribed standard, it is important to note that IT comprises different functional segments and each segment comes with its own "flavor." Grouping everything into one box without systematic thinking will relegate IT only to a support role. By pigeonholing a library's IT department into a support role, organizations are likely to miss out on invaluable contributions from talented IT staff. Libraries can more fully engage with technology by empowering their most fluent practitioners and by positioning the IT department at the core of libraries' strategic priorities rather than relegating the technology function to the fringes. Open source initiatives such as Hydra or Koha are good examples of how technology can drive innovations in core library operations.

The Gartner report, through its ITScore, lays out the expectations that enterprises have of IT's contribution on a sliding scale—functional, enabling, contributing, differentiating, transformational. At the functional level (ITScore level 1), enterprises view IT as a commodity and a necessary cost of business, but see little potential in it beyond basic task automation. At this level, enterprise leaders expect it to be invisible, available, and reliable. At the enabling level (ITScore level 2), enterprises expect IT to enable and potentially improve back-office business operations. At the contributing level (ITScore level 3), enterprises have matured to a proactive and collaborative relationship with IT, primarily focused on business operational improvements through performance management and process engineering. At the differentiating level (ITScore level 4), enterprises seek to dominate their industries, strategically employing IT as a differentiator for their key value propositions. At transformational level (ITScore level 5), enterprises use IT to redefine markets, industries, and competition. At this maturity level, IT is an innovation engine dedicated to creative destruction, transformation, and strategic change (Gartner 2016, 5). This scale indicates the maturity level of the enterprise in relation to its IT strategy. If one were to map the IT operations' demands on one axis and their corresponding expectations on the other axis, one may imagine some variant of the graph shown in figure 9.1.

Figure 9.1 captures the IT operations and the expectations from the enterprise in one place. It can also be viewed as a good representation of business strategy as it relates to IT operations. The values on the independent axis (x-axis) can be populated by internal IT departments weighing each functional area with respect to whether it is a common commodity service that can be sourced from elsewhere or whether it is something very unique that only libraries could offer. Examples on the commodity (common) side include networking and identity management whereas examples on the other extreme include new and emerging functional areas such as research data management and digital preservation. Another useful way to think about the progres-

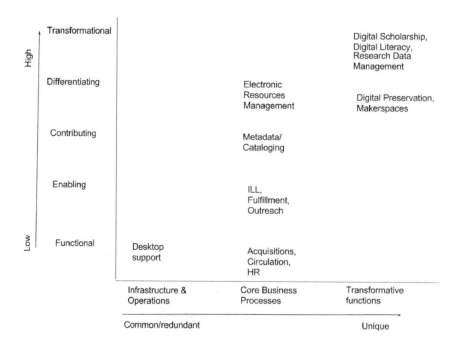

Figure 9.1.   The IT operations of the library in terms of business strategy.

sion of values on the x-axis—as we move along with the axis, the IT services shift from "services to run the business" to "services of the business"; for example, networking, computer/desktop support, and so forth, are essential IT services for any business to run their internal operations, whereas services such as digital preservation are more of an offering from the library for its users. The values on the y-axis reflect a sliding scale of increasing expectations of IT from the enterprise. IT leaders need to facilitate discussions with the leadership to understand their expectations and design the IT structure to deliver on these expectations. Domain experts from the functional areas where the enterprise expects IT to be transformative need to work very closely with IT experts.

Implications of the structure: There are many different forms of organizational structure, but the common ones include functional, divisional, matrix-like, hybrid, and process oriented (Iochpe and Thom 2001). The functional structure focuses on practical specialization whereby similar or related occupational specialties are grouped together (also referred to as departmentalization). For example, grouping catalogers together as one department in the library. A divisional structure gives larger companies the capacity to separate large sections of the business into semiautonomous units or divisions. For example, treating archives or special collections as a separate division within the library since the activities and workflows in those areas can sometimes be autonomous (acquiring donations, hosting special exhibits). A matrix-like organizational structure is a company structure in which the reporting relationships are set up as a grid, or matrix, rather than in the traditional hierarchy (Hartzell 2016). For example, a programmer may be part of the IT department but spends most of his or her time assisting in digital scholarship work and participating in different departments' meetings. Hybrid (mix of multiple organizational design structures) and process-oriented structures (where the emphasis is on business processes) round up the many forms of organizational structure. The IT operations–business strategy diagram (figure 9.1) will help guide a discussion on how potential points on the diagram can map to functional, divisional, and matrix-like structures.

The overall strategy for IT should be to make investments in human resources that appear at the upper right corner of the diagram (demands of IT are high because that type of work could potentially be done only locally and expectations from the enterprise are at a high level). This type of thinking is consistent with the thinking that others have proposed in terms of future library direction—one that does not pigeonhole library or librarians' work into a purely service role in the minds of scholars (Brunner 2010; Bennett 2009). If the future of the library is in developing products, then IT will be undoubtedly a core part of it. Investing in human resources is both a rewarding and expensive endeavor. Care should be taken to manage investment in human resources so that redundant and duplicative services (from an entire organization's perspective) are eliminated wherever feasible.

An infrastructure and operations group can be a stand-alone functional unit of IT as the expectations from the library from these operations might be at a pure support level (functional, on the y-axis which is the lowest level). Basic computing and networking services are needed to run any business, and within academic library settings, every division or department will need these services. It is likely that such services may be outsourced to a central campus IT unit where feasible (depending on cost structure and SLAs). But if these services are to be provided locally, then the infrastructure and operations group can be tasked with running these services. Though the skills needed to provision a desktop are much different than skills needed to run and monitor a network, because of the relatively well-defined nature of work and small number of IT administrators needed to run such services, it is much more efficient to group these services together as a functional unit.

When the expectations from the enterprise are enabling or contributing (middle of the scale), then, of the three structures being considered, either functional or matrix-like structure might turn out to be a preferred option. Depending on the size of the IT team (large), size of the overall organization (large), specific demands (high), and comfort level of management to pursue matrix-like structure (well trained in matrix structures, managing dual reporting lines, performance management is set to handle dual reporting lines, etc.), a matrix-like structure might work well. If the IT programmers are few in number and programming resources cannot be dedicated to a specific organizational function, then a functional structure where all the programmers are grouped in one unit could be considered. Ideally, programmers working in close proximity with the subject-matter experts would be positioned to develop great products (matrix-like structure). This would also help them gain necessary subject-matter knowledge. For example, a developer who consistently works with digital humanities/digital scholarship–related projects are much more likely to develop an understanding of scholars' needs in those areas than someone who may have to juggle between general programming tasks and domain-specific projects.

If the organization expects IT to be differentiating or transformational, then either a matrix-like structure or the divisional structure (with the IT experts at the helm) might be considered. Division structure is mainly based on the semiautonomous nature of the work rather than the number of employees, and it might fit very well in cases where an organization wants to explore a new direction, for example, to figure out the role of the library in the research data management domain. In areas where the organization expects IT to be a transformative force, then those areas need to be led by IT professionals, as the expectations need to match the responsibilities.

CONCLUSION

It is very important to align technology with business strategy and structure. While there is no exact science to figure out the sliding scale for an enterprise's expectations of IT or the exact number of demands that can be articulated of IT, constant communication between IT and library leaders is a must. Together, the leadership needs to settle on a local strategy and consider the technology's impact on the structure. Library IT leaders need to proactively engage their deans and directors in discussions about expectations of IT and design solutions to match those expectations. If the library leadership expects IT to be an enabler of business functions, then the IT structure, strategy, and technologies need to reflect that. A framework to tie these three important things together (strategy, structure, and technology) was discussed in this chapter—though it is not a prescriptive model by any means, library IT leaders could use the model as a conversation starter with their leadership and develop broad strategies for their organizations. In this environment of increasing economic pressure, doing more with less has become the norm. By tapping the most fluent IT practitioners to lead innovative services, libraries can fully engage with technology. For organizations that are interested in moving IT from periphery to the core, the answer lies not in reorganizing and restructuring alone but in changing the attitude so a shift happens from library as purely a service provider to library also as a product developer.

REFERENCES

Askey, Dale, and Lisa Janicke Hinchliffe. 2016. "From Invasive to Integrated: Information Technology and Library Leadership, Structure, and Culture." Project briefing presented at the CNI Spring 2016 Membership Meeting, San Antonio, Tex., April 4–5.

Auckland, Mary. 2012. "Re-skilling for Research: An Investigation into the Role and Skills of Subject and Liaison Librarians Required to Effectively Support the Evolving Information Needs of Researchers." *RLUK Report*. Accessed June 25, 2015. http://www.rluk.ac.uk/wp-content/uploads/2014/02/RLUK-Re-skilling.pdf.

Bennett, Scott. 2009. "Libraries and Learning: A History of Paradigm Change." *portal: Libraries and the Academy* 9 (2): 181–97.

Bergeron, François, Louis Raymond, and Suzanne Rivard. 2004. "Ideal Patterns of Strategic Alignment and Business Performance." *Information & Management* 41 (8): 1003–20.

Bowen, William G. 2012. "The 'Cost Disease' in Higher Education: Is Technology the Answer?" The Tanner Lectures, Stanford University.

Breeding, Marshall. 2007. "It's Time to Break the Mold of the Original ILS." *Computers in Libraries* 27 (10): 39–41.

———. 2013. "Library Technology: The Next Generation." *Computers in Libraries* 33 (8), 16–18.

Brophy, Peter, and Peter Wynne. 1997. *Management Information Systems and Performance Measurement for the Electronic Library: eLib Supporting Study (MIEL2) Final Report.*

Brunner, M. L. 2010. "PhD Holders in the Academic Library: The CLIR Postdoctoral Fellowship Program." In *The Expert Library: Staffing, Sustaining, and Advancing the Academic Library in the 21st Century*, edited by S. Walter and K. Williams, 158–89. Chicago: Association of College & Research Libraries.

Doherty, Neil F., Donna Champion, and Leitao Wang. 2010. "An Holistic Approach to Understanding the Changing Nature of Organisational Structure." *Information Technology & People* 23 (2): 116–35.

Farhanghi, Ali Akbar, Abbas Abbaspour, and Reza Abachian Ghassemi. 2013. "The Effect of Information Technology on Organizational Structure and Firm Performance: An Analysis of Consultant Engineers Firms (CEF) in Iran." *Procedia-Social and Behavioral Sciences* 81: 644–49.

Fu, Ping, and Moira Fitzgerald. 2013. "A Comparative Analysis of the Effect of the Integrated Library System on Staffing Models in Academic Libraries." *Information Technology and Libraries* 32 (3).

Gartner. 2016. "Renewing the IT Organizational Model Primer for 2016." March 11.

Gibson, Craig, and Christopher Dixon. 2011. "New Metrics for Academic Library Engagement." In *A Declaration of Interdependence—ACRL Conference March*, 340–51.

Hartzell, Sherri. 2016. "Types of Traditional Organizational Designs: Simple, Functional & Divisional Designs." Study.com, n.d. Accessed June 29, 2016. http://study.com/academy/lesson/types-of-organizational-structures-functional-divisional-matrix-team-network.html.

Heider, Kelly L., Sandra Janicki, Joann Janosko, Blaine Knupp, and Carl Rahkonen. 2012. "Faculty Perceptions of the Value of Academic Libraries: A Mixed Method Study." *Library Philosophy and Practice*, Paper 909. http://digitalcommons.unl.edu/libphilprac/909.

Henry, Tyce, Ernesto Pagano, J. Puckett, and Joanne Wilson. 2014. "Five Trends to Watch in Higher Education." Boston Consulting Group, April.

Iochpe, Cirano, and Lucinéia Heloisa Thom. 2001. "Relying on the Organizational Structure to Model Workflow Processes." *ICEIS* 2: 740–44.

Jaggars, Damon E. 2014. "We Can Imagine the Future, but Are We Equipped to Create It?" *portal: Libraries and the Academy* 14 (3): 319–23.

Jones, Spencer S., Paul S. Heaton, Robert S. Rudin, and Eric C. Schneider. 2012. "Unraveling the IT Productivity Paradox—Lessons for Health Care." *New England Journal of Medicine* 366 (24): 2243–45.

Kinner, Laura, and Christine Rigda. 2009. "The Integrated Library System: From Daring to Dinosaur?" *Journal of Library Administration* 49 (4): 401–17. doi:10.1080/01930820902832546.

Long, Matthew P., and Roger C. Schonfeld. 2014. "Ithaka S+R US Library Survey 2013." Ithaka S+R.

Lynch, Clifford. 2000. "From Automation to Transformation." *Educause Review* 35 (1): 60–69.

Mokyr, Joel. 1992. *The Lever of Riches: Technological Creativity and Economic Progress.* Oxford: Oxford University Press.

Munn, Robert F. 1968. "The Bottomless Pit, or the Academic Library as Viewed from the Administration Building." *College & Research Libraries* 29 (1): 51–54.

New Media Consortium. 2014. *NMC Horizon Report: 2014 Higher Education Edition.*

Orlikowski, Wanda J. 1992. "The Duality of Technology: Rethinking the Concept of Technology in Organizations." *Organization Science* 3 (3): 398–427.

Rose, Jeremy, and Matthew Jones. 2005. "The Double Dance of Agency: A Socio-theoretic Account of How Machines and Humans Interact." *Systems, Signs & Actions* 1 (1): 19–37.

Troll, Denise A. 2002. "How and Why Libraries Are Changing: What We Know and What We Need to Know." *portal: Libraries and the Academy* 2 (1): 99–123.

FURTHER READING

Barney, Jay B., and Ricky W. Griffin. 1992. *The Management of Organizations: Strategy, Structure, Behavior.* Boston: Houghton Mifflin College Division.

Moore, Susan. 2016. "Gartner Highlights Top 10 Strategic Technologies for Higher Education in 2016." Gartner, February 25. https://www.gartner.com/newsroom/id/3225717.

Stoffle, Carla J., Robert Renaud, and Jerilyn R. Veldof. 1996. "Choosing Our Futures." *College & Research Libraries* 57 (3): 213–25.

Index

About the Editors and Contributors

Dr. Carl Antonucci is director of library services, Elihu Burritt Library, Central Connecticut State University in New Britain, Connecticut. He has been employed in library services in higher education since 1993. He currently serves as the Connecticut chapter councilor to the American Library Association and serves as the cochair of the Legislative Committee of the Connecticut Library Association. He has had many leadership roles in library associations and has served as the president of the Connecticut Library Association and the chair of the board of directors of the Connecticut Library Consortium. He has a doctorate in history from Providence College and has a master's in library science from Simmons College. Dr. Antonucci's dissertation is on machine politics and urban renewal in Providence, Rhode Island, during the era of Mayor Joseph Doorley. His other areas of interests include Italian American studies, and he has published the following papers with Professor Kenneth DiMaggio: "When Russo Street was Mussolini Street: Revisiting an Apocryphal Chapter in the Italian American Cultural Narrative," "The Dictator Stays in the Picture: The Forgotten History of a Controversial Mural," and "Son of Italy, Stepson of Sisyphus: Re-appraising the Immigrant Experience as Existential Dilemma." Dr. Antonucci and Professor DiMaggio are currently working on a critical biography of the pick-and-shovel poet Pascal D'Angelo. The book will be published in 2017. Dr. Antonucci and Sharon Clapp also have published a chapter in *Leading the 21st-Century Academic Library: Successful Strategies for Envisioning and Realizing Preferred Futures*, published by Rowman & Littlefield in 2015.

Sharon Clapp is the digital resources librarian at the Elihu Burritt Library, Central Connecticut State University in New Britain, Connecticut. Sharon has trained and supported library staff on integrated library systems, virtual reference, website development, and user experience design since 1998 and has recently expanded her work to include building students' digital literacy within the information literacy framework. She received her baccalaureate in anthropology, graduating Phi Beta Kappa from Mount Holyoke College in 1998, then took a position working with library technology for the nonprofit Bibliomation Library Consortium in Connecticut. She received her master's in library/information science from Southern Connecticut State University, managed a county library information technology department in California, then returned to Connecticut where she worked as a web developer at the State Library. She took the position as digital resources librarian at Central Connecticut State University's Elihu Burritt Library in 2013. Working with Dr. Carl Antonucci, she has published work on strategic planning and change in the twenty-first-century academic library. They also presented a session on the "Librarian as Leader, Entrepreneur, and Technologist" at the 2014 LITA National Forum, which served as the basis for this book. Sharon is passionately concerned about user experience design and digital literacy, as well as being an advocate for the use of open educational resources and for library participation in open source software projects. She is an active avocational archaeologist and trustee for the Institute for American Indian Studies Museum & Research Center in Washington, Connecticut.

* * *

Caitlin A. Bagley is an assistant professor and instruction librarian at Gonzaga University. She received her MLS from Indiana University. She is the author of *Makerspaces: Top Trailblazing Projects* and has also been published in *Introduction to Cloud Computing: A LITA Guide and Social Information Research*. She is interested in the intersection between technology and education, and firmly believes libraries and librarians should be leaders in this area. She lives in Spokane, Washington.

Dean of the UT Arlington Libraries since 2012, **Rebecca Bichel** leads a team of 115 full-time and 150 student employees. Since 2013, UTA Libraries has been on an ambitious journey to transform into the model twenty-first-century urban research university library. The libraries' strategy is centered on disruptive innovation, data-driven decision making, quality user experiences, and university-centered planning. Before coming to UTA, Rebecca served at Florida State and Penn State University Libraries, among others. She earned her master of library information science degree from the University of Hawaii at Manoa.

Michael A. Crumpton, MLS, SHRM-SCP, is the assistant dean for administrative services at the University of North Carolina at Greensboro. Mike oversees administration of budgets, human resources, and facilities, and organizes and addresses space and remodeling issues. He is an adjunct instructor for the Department of Library and Information Studies at the University of North Carolina at Greensboro. He is certified as a senior human resources professional and also holds a graduate certificate in adult teaching. His published works can be viewed at http://libres.uncg.edu/ir/uncg/clist.aspx?id=1946.

Emy Nelson Decker is the NextGen public services manager for the Georgia Tech Library. She holds an MLIS from Valdosta State University and an MA in art history from the University of Chicago. Emy's current interests are centered on reimagining public services toward a greater focus on user engagement and the needs of digital thinkers. In addition to presenting in venues such as the American Library Association and the Association of College & Research Libraries, she has published numerous refereed journal articles and book chapters within the library field.

Bradford Lee Eden is dean of library services at Valparaiso University. He has both a master's and a PhD in musicology, as well as an MS in library science. His recent books include *Middle-Earth Minstrel: Essays on Music in Tolkien* (2010); *The Associate University Librarian Handbook: A Resource Guide* (Scarecrow Press, 2012); *Leadership in Academic Libraries: Connecting Theory to Practice* (Scarecrow Press, 2014); *The Hobbit and Tolkien's Mythology: Essays on Revisions and Influences* (2014), and the ten-volume series Creating the 21st-Century Academic Library (Rowman & Littlefield, 2015–2017).

Marlee Givens is strategic initiatives manager for the Georgia Tech Library. In this role she has managed a variety of projects to support the library's strategic objectives, including campus engagement and outreach, reaffirmation of Georgia Tech's accreditation, and training assessment, development, and delivery. She has presented at state and national conferences on project management and scholarly communication, and taught workshops on library technologies and evaluating library services. Marlee holds an MLS from the University of Maryland and an MA in French from the University of Georgia.

Bruce Henson is the associate dean for research and learning services at the Georgia Tech Library, where he has worked since 1998, and has served in roles including liaison librarian and the head of reference. He holds an MLS from the University of North Carolina at Chapel Hill and a BA in history from Mary Baldwin College with a historic preservation minor.

Hong Ma is head of library systems at Loyola University in Chicago. She is a regular writer and speaker on implementing large-scale digital projects and systems. She is also active in the Library Information Technology Association (LITA).

Harish Maringanti started his career in libraries as a staff programmer at Kansas State University Libraries, managing various systems including digital repositories and subsequently managing a team responsible for desktop support, application development, and system administration. In his current role as the associate dean for IT and digital library services (librarian) at J. Willard Marriott Library, he is responsible for advancing the library's technology initiatives including strategy, policies, compliance, business processes, and infrastructure. His educational background includes an MS in computing and information sciences and a graduate certificate in organizational leadership, both from Kansas State.

Michael Rodriguez is an electronic resources librarian at the University of Connecticut in Storrs. He specializes in licensing and acquisitions, project management, and digital innovation generally. Before joining UConn, he served as e-learning librarian at Hodges University and as a circulation and reference assistant at Collier County Public Library, in Florida. Michael earned his MLIS from Florida State University in 2014. In 2015, he was named a Library Journal Reviewer of the Year. In his spare time, Michael blogs and tweets for the Library Information Technology Association (LITA).

C. Heather Scalf earned her master of library and information science degree from the University of North Texas. She has been with the UT Arlington Libraries since 2005 and has served in various leadership roles within the organization. In her current role, she is responsible for all assessment reporting, as well as the development of future qualitative and quantitative assessment tools to support and evaluate a variety of initiatives within the libraries. She has also served at the United States Military Academy at West Point and at Mary Baldwin College in Virginia.

Mary G. Scanlon is the research and instruction librarian for business and economics at Wake Forest University. She earned her MBA at the Weatherhead School of Management at Case Western Reserve University and her MLIS at Kent State University. At Wake Forest, she serves as liaison and subject specialist in the School of Business along with the Department of Economics and the minor in entrepreneurship and social enterprise. She holds a bachelor's degree in biology and has indulged a lifelong interest in gardening. She is currently developing her backyard into a wildlife habitat by planting native plants in a chemical-free environment.

Junior Tidal (jtidal@citytech.cuny.edu) is multimedia and web services librarian and associate professor for the Ursula C. Schwerin Library at the New York City College of Technology, CUNY. He has published in the *Journal of Web Librarianship*, *Computers in Libraries*, and *code4Lib Journal*. In 2015, he authored a LITA guide titled *Usability and the Mobile Web*. He has presented at the ALA Annual Conference, National LITA Forum, and ACRL National Conference. Originally from Whitesburg, Kentucky, he has earned an MLS and a master's in information science from Indiana University.